THE MESSAGE
OF FOSSILS

PASCAL

TASSY

THE MESSAGE

OF FOSSILS

McGraw-Hill, Inc.

New York St. Louis San Francisco Auckland Bogotá
Caracas Lisbon London Madrid Mexico
Milan Montreal New Delhi Paris
San Juan São Paulo Singapore
Sydney Tokyo Toronto

English Language Edition

Translated by Nicholas Hartmann
in collaboration with
The Language Service, Inc.
Poughkeepsie, New York

Typography by AB Typesetting
Poughkeepsie, New York

Library of Congress Cataloging-in-Publication Data
Tassy, Pascal.
[*Message des fossiles*. English]
The message of fossils / Pascal Tassy.
p. cm. — (The McGraw-Hill HORIZONS OF SCIENCE series)
Translation of: *Le Message des fossiles*.
Includes bibliographical references.
ISBN 0-07-062947-1
1. Fossils. 2. Evolution (Biology). I. Title. II. Series.
QE711.2.T3713   1993   92-46671
560 — dc20

The original French language edition of this book
was published as *Le Message des fossiles*, copyright © 1991,
Hachette, Paris, France.
Questions de science series
Series editor, Dominique Lecourt

 This book is printed on recycled, acid-free paper containing a minimum of 50% recycled de-
inked fiber.

TABLE OF CONTENTS

INTRODUCTION

It was not until the end of the 18th century that the term "fossil" was used to designate the remains of living organisms preserved in rocks. Until then, in accordance with its Latin etymology (*fodere* = to dig), it referred indifferently to anything extracted from the Earth that was likely to arouse interest and curiosity. As late as 1761, in his treatise *De La Nature* [On Nature], Jean-Baptiste Robinet (1735–1820) referred to "the animal nature of metals, stones, and all sorts of fossil substances," which might just as well be minerals or various concretions. Could this linguistic imprecision perhaps be attributed to a certain lack of interest in the painstaking observation of Nature?

A consideration of the many accounts that have come down to us from Greek and Roman antiquity suggests that such was not the case. Indeed in later centuries a true passion was expressed for some of the discoveries that would later be understood in the context of what we now call "geology." It is of course anachronistic to imagine that either "geology" or "paleontology" existed in Antiquity; the very words themselves, like their contemporary "biology," did not appear until the beginning of the 19th century.

We do know, however, that Xenophanes of Colophon
(ca. 560–478 B.C.) had observed the presence of
seashells far inland, and indeed on mountainsides; he
had noted the imprints left by fish and seaweeds in
the quarries of Syracuse, Paros, and Malta.

These observations, also made by Herodotus
(ca. 484–420 B.C.), repeated by Xenophon (ca. 430–
ca. 355 B.C.), and confirmed by Plutarch (ca. 46–ca.
120 A.D.), found a powerful echo in a few often-
cited lines of the great Latin poet Ovid (ca. 43 B.C.–
17 A.D.), in Book 15 of his *Metamorphoses*: "I
myself have seen what once was most solid earth
become sea; I have seen land born from the waves;
and the soil, far from the sea, is often strewn with
seashells [...]"

These shells and these imprints therefore
"spoke" to the ancients. Neither Xenophanes nor
Herodotus had misread the gist of the message: in the
past, the oceans had extended well beyond their
observed limits. Two of the most famous geogra-
phers of Antiquity had moreover proposed different
explanations for these movements of the sea. The
first was Eratosthenes (ca. 276–194 B.C.), a contemporary of Archimedes who lived in the 3rd century
B.C., and whose fame rests on the fact that he measured the circumference of the Earth. According to
him, the level of the Mediterranean Sea had dropped
due to the sudden opening of the two straits that
marked its boundaries: the "Pillars of Hercules"

(Straits of Gibraltar) that opened into the Atlantic, and the Euxine Pontus (Bosporus) through which it communicated with the Black Sea.

Mere illusion, replied the second geographer four centuries later. Setting out in search of "true causes" identifiable in present-day Nature, Strabo (ca. 64 B.C.–ca. 23 A.D.) described the earthquakes, volcanic eruptions, elevations of the sea bed, and subsidences and landslides that had actually occurred. In his immense *Geography*, he stated that the presence of seashells far from the seashore was attributable to tidal waves.

The fact remains that this message from the fossils was difficult to reconcile with the ancient concept of the Earth. This no doubt explains the fact, often remarked upon, that no mention is made of fossils in the works of Aristotle (384–322 B.C.), otherwise so encyclopedic and so rich in concrete observation. His cosmology, however, is based on an eternal Universe in which the terrestrial world, although subject to change (like all of the "sublunary" world), did not experience the sudden movements implied by Xenophanes' interpretation of the distribution of fossils.

Somewhat paradoxically, the centuries-long predominance of Aristotle's view of the world thus gave full rein to the imagination of natural scientists (and a very fertile imagination it was). Since the message of the fossils could not be understood rationally by relating it to some natural process or event, it tended to acquire supernatural overtones. Pliny the Elder (23–79 A.D.), pondering the origin of what we now know to be fossil shark's teeth, already saw in them a resemblance to the human tongue. They therefore acquired the name of "glossopetra" (literally, stone tongues, or if you prefer, "tongue-stones"). What is more, the author of the *Historia Naturalis* did not hesitate to state that they fell from the sky during eclipses of the Moon. This legend came down through the Middle Ages, transmuted into a religious context. Dubbed "Saint Paul's tongues," these glossopetra would be regarded as the petrified remains of the tongues belonging to the snakes which, according to legend, the apostle had placed under a curse after one of them had bitten him during his sojourn on the island of Malta. These shark's teeth, in their guise as snake's teeth, would thus be considered to have particular medicinal properties, especially—via a process of semantic contamination common in magical thinking—that of absorbing and neutralizing venoms and poisons.

The same type of magical thinking immediately seized upon the remains of fossil mammals discovered in antiquity. Empedocles (ca. 492–ca. 432 B.C.) describes the discovery of huge bones in Sicily, and sees in them the vestiges of the mythical race of "giants" whose features had first been outlined by Homer. The legend was passed on to Rome, and persisted down to the 17th century, once again becoming entangled with religious beliefs of Christian origin. Saint Christopher, who was said to have been unusually tall, thus became associated with a mammoth molar and the dorsal vertebra of an elephant, preserved and venerated as relics in Valencia and Munich, respectively. In the Carpathian and Transylvanian regions, as in China, there developed a "dragon" mythology centered around the remains of the great Quaternary mammals, while the mysterious and fascinating unicorn, diverging in the popular imagination from the single-horned rhinoceros of India, inspired the fantasies of medieval Europe. Its single horn was believed to have the same curative properties as those of the glossopetra, in some cases along with powerful aphrodisiac powers. A lively trade in putative unicorn horns promptly arose and flourished.

It was not until the end of the 16th century that some began to question these fables. Ambroise Paré (1510–1590) published, in 1580, a *Discours sur la licorne* [Discourse on the unicorn] to denounce these fantasies. A century later the Jesuit Athanasius Kircher (1601–1680) weighed in against the "giants." Does this indicate that the move was on towards a better understanding of the message of fossils, as certain linear concepts of the progress of human knowledge might lead us to believe? Not at all, since it was the organic nature and origin of fossils that was suddenly questioned, to be replaced by a mysterious "plastic force" believed to be at work within the rocks, playfully imitating living forms. Such was the opinion of Kircher in his famous *Mundus subterraneus* [Subterranean world] (1665), and also that of the physician Gabriele Falloppio (1523–1562), who unhesitatingly interpreted the fossil elephants discovered in Italy as stone concretions!

The idea that fossils were organic in origin did not really become established until the very end of the 17th century, even though (as we have seen) by then it could not be considered novel. It had even come back into favor during the Renaissance. Leonardo da Vinci (1452–1519) had reaffirmed it, and Bernard Le Bovier de Fontenelle (1657–1757) sang the praises of Bernard Palissy (1510–1589) with these words: "A simple potter who knew neither Latin nor Greek was the first who dared to say, in Paris towards the end of the 16th century, and in defiance of all the learned scholars, that fossil shells were real shells deposited long ago by the sea in places where they lived, while animals, and especially fish, had given the "figured stones" all their different shapes; and he bravely challenged the entire school of Aristotle to refute his proof." Even though Voltaire at this same period continued to argue that fossils represented mere "sports of Nature," the naturalists of the 18th century, led by Buffon (1707–1788) in his *Théorie de la Terre* [Theory of the Earth] in 1749, had confirmed the "organic" theory and had added, following the lead of the philosopher G. W. Leibniz (1646–1716) in his *Protogea*, that "in the great changes that the world has undergone, a great number of animal forms have been transformed." Buffon went even further, asserting that certain fossils obviously belonged to "animals which once existed and no longer do."

The revival and then the victory of this thesis can without doubt be regarded as indirect consequences of the dismemberment of Aristotelian physics and the beginnings of modern science. But three other currents, of considerable historical importance, were also at work. The first had to do with the accumulation and diversification of evidence, revealed by progress in mining activities and the exploration of new territories. The second was the improvement in observational techniques; for example, Robert Hooke (1635–1703), one of the pillars of the Royal Society founded in 1606, was able clearly to discern "petrified" animals and plants in crystals by using the newly invented microscope. The third factor, paradoxically, was the theological squabble that this thesis inevitably provoked. The Protestant Reformation had encouraged a literal reading of the Bible, raising the question of how to reconcile the fossil message with the word of Holy Scripture. As a result, the Flood was long a focus for lively dispute. The book of Genesis described a universal, instantaneous, and violent event. Could it not easily explain the presence of seashells on mountains, since marine animals had at that moment been carried off and transported by the force of the waters? There was a small difficulty of chronology, however, since the literal reading of Genesis worked out by Bishop James Ussher was considered authoritative. In 1654, based on calculations of stupefying precision, Ussher had announced that the Earth had been created on October 26 of the year 4004 before Christ! To many naturalists, this span of time seemed much too short to account for the history that fossils now seemed to embody. But at least the continuing debate encouraged the collection and description of fossil materials.

With the publication by Georges Cuvier (1769–1832) of his *Discours sur les révolutions de la surface du globe et sur les changements qu'elles ont produits dans le règne animal* [Discourse concerning the revolutions of the surface of the globe, and the changes which they have produced in the animal kingdom], the question of fossils took on a definitively modern meaning. This text originally constituted the preface to a monumental work entitled *Recherches sur les ossements fossiles des quadrupèdes* [Research concerning the fossil bones of the quadrupeds]. Its grand style made it so successful that it was later republished individually, translated into every European language, and then re-issued numerous times. This Discourse and this book mark the scientific debut of comparative anatomy, of which animal "paleontology"—the word was not coined until 1832, by H. de Blainville—would for a while constitute one branch. The task now became to establish relationships between fossilized remains and rock strata, a discipline called "stratigraphy" whose beginnings can be dated to the work of the Dane Niels Stensen (Nicolaus Steno) (1638–1686).

One partisan, caricaturing school of history has long painted Cuvier as the representative of the Crown and the Church, although he was in fact a Lutheran. He is contrasted with the personality of Jean-Baptiste de Monet, Chevalier de Lamarck (1744–1829), his unfortunate colleague and rival at the Muséum d'Histoire Naturelle in Paris, defender of the ideals of the French Revolution. The story is that Cuvier, an Imperial baron coddled by the powers that be, triumphed over Lamarck thanks to his political connections. We are shown the pious image of Lamarck dying blind and penniless, unaware of his posthumous glory to come, and led to believe that Cuvier's theory was retrograde—were not his "revolutions" indistinguishable from "catastrophes"? —while Lamarck's was progressive. The misunderstanding was even more seductive given that the author of the *Philosophie zoologique* [Zoological philosophy] (1809) presented a vision of the "transformations" of species as a kind of "progress" made by life in its struggle with the physical environment. Forced to make "adaptations" imposed by that environment, which were then transmitted as an "acquisition" from one generation to the next, life represented an ascendant force continually aiming towards increasing perfection.

Cuvier's scientific work, which owed much to his teacher, Johann Friedrich Blumenbach (1752–1840), a professor at Jena in Germany, appears in a very different light: its "catastrophism" emerges by no means as the expression of some unshakable religious dogmatism, but rather as the conclusion drawn from methodical observations by a scholar who invoked the name of Newton: "Doubtless the astronomers have advanced more quickly than the naturalists, and the present state of the theory of the Earth bears some resemblance to a time in which certain philosophers believed the heavens to be made of stone, or the Moon to be as big as the Peloponnesus; but after Anaxagoras came Copernicus and Kepler who paved the way for Newton; and why should not natural history some day also have its Newton?" The word "revolution" betrays this ambition; after the revolutions of the heavenly bodies elucidated in Newton's cosmological system, here are revolutions which occur "on the surface of the Earth." "Antiquarian of a new species, [Cuvier must] both restore [the] monuments of past revolutions and [...] decipher their meaning." This "restoration," which made him famous overnight, was based on a method of his own invention — called "comparative anatomy" — which consisted in considering (like a good Newtonian) that "every organized being forms an assemblage, a single, closed system, whose parts mutually correspond and participate in the same definitive action by means of a reciprocal reaction. None of these parts can change unless the others also change; and consequently each of them, taken separately, indicates and yields all the others." For example, if an animal's intestines are organized so as only to digest recently killed meat, "its jaws must be constructed to devour prey; its claws to seize and tear it; its teeth to cut and divide it; and the entire system of its organs of movement to pursue and capture it [...]."

This correlation principle, which allowed him to formulate the first "general laws" of comparative anatomy, was accompanied by a connection principle stated by Étienne Geoffroy Saint-Hilaire in 1818, according to which a particular organ can be recognized in different species regardless of its form or function: a particular organ always has a constant situational relationship to any other given organ.

Whether it was true or not, Cuvier gained the reputation of being able to reconstruct an entire animal from a single bone.

If the results of this restoration are correlated with geological observations, they reveal (according to Cuvier) a remarkable succession of closed worlds, completely separated from one another by sudden and destructive events, or "catastrophes." The work of restoration therefore suggests the idea of revolution. This explains the existence of 90 unknown species discovered by Cuvier: these were species that had been destroyed during these great upheavals that he referred to as "horrible," perhaps not without some political malice. The biblical Flood appears in this scenario only as the last of these catastrophes in a long series of events of the same type, or, in the author's own words, "the last universal inundation," the only one of which popular tradition retained any memory. In northern regions it left the corpses of the great quadrupeds, entombed by the ice, preserved down to our own day with their skin, fur, and flesh. "If they had not been frozen as soon as they died, putrefaction would have decomposed them. And on the other hand this eternal frost was not previously present in the places where they were struck down, since they would not have been able to live at such temperatures. The event that killed the animals and made their habitat glacial was thus one and the same."

Cuvier thus distinguishes a number of successive epochs. The most ancient landscapes contain invertebrates (molluscs and crustaceans) and fish.

Then come the reptiles and the mammals, first in marine forms (cetaceans) and finally land mammals. In this way he gathers up the various theories of the Earth that had prevailed since the end of the 17th century, from the *Telluris Theoria Sacra* [Sacred theory of the Earth] published by Thomas Burnet in 1681, to Buffon's *Théorie de la Terre* [Theory of the Earth] (1749), not forgetting the *Essays on natural history* of John Woodward (1665–1728) which appeared in London in 1702. Cuvier will have nothing to do with Burnet's intention, which was to confirm the biblical account using the methods and concepts of the natural sciences. On the contrary, he regards the Earth's history as "thousands of centuries" old, although he is still discreet about the matter. But unlike Lamarck, who challenged the idea of vanished species, Cuvier rejects the idea of the transformation of species, and also does not bother to discuss the examples of transformation studied by Lamarck with reference to invertebrate shells. He never tires of emphasizing that the fossil record nowhere displays the "intermediate forms" implied by the continuous evolution of life described by Lamarck in his *Philosophie zoologique* (1809).

Henceforth paleontologists would focus their efforts on defining the meaning of the message of the fossils. It is an irony of history that the geological lessons which were of such assistance to Cuvier as he spelled out the first words would later come back to confuse the text for decades. A double paradox: it was by establishing its own scientific foundations that geology managed to produce this counter-effect.

Stephen Jay Gould has given an admirable description of these contradictory trends in his book *Time's Arrow — Time's Cycle*. Charles Lyell (1797–1875), author of the *Principles of Geology* (1830), emerges as the "hero" of this story, for it was he who established two essential methodological principles. According to the first, it is possible to understand phenomena that occurred in the past by simply comparing the traces they have left with present-day phenomena that we can observe directly. This principle encompasses the idea of the constancy or immutability of natural laws over space and time. It was subsequently summarized in an adage too general not to be equivocal: "the present is the key to the past." In an article published in 1832, William Whewell (1794–1866) gave it a name—"uniformitarianism"—that has stood the test of time and at least has the virtue of not possessing any teleological overtones. The second principle, often referred to as "actualism," offers a refurbished version of the traditional "simplicity principle"; in other words, do not invent superfluous causes when the observable phenomena speak for themselves.

But with the help of these two principles and some rhetorical artifices, Lyell gained acceptance for another, very different thesis: that the causes acting in the past have never ceased to be operative, and with a constant intensity. This yields a representation of geological change as slow, regular, and gradual. In the name of this "gradualist" principle, Lyell heaps scorn on Cuvier and the catastrophists. In the course of the eleven reissues of his book over more than forty years, he managed (at least in the English-speaking countries) to impose the idea that gradualism represented the only scientific concept of the history of the Earth, and that any notion of catastrophe must be attributed to some religious belief, whether stated or more or less expertly concealed.

When Charles Darwin (1809–1882) embarked on the *Beagle* in 1831 for the voyage that would take him to the coasts of South America and carry him around the world, he brought Lyell's book with him. This work was a critical factor in guiding first his observations, and then the interpretations that he later gave to them. It was to Lyell that the young naturalist owed his interest (pivotal in many respects) in the geographical distribution of species and in their isolation: the *Principles* stated, after all, that each species had developed in specific regions, each arising from an original focus. Lyell had borrowed this idea from the founder of "historical biogeography," the Swiss naturalist Augustin-Pyrame de Candolle (1778–1841). We also know, however, that the Darwinian theory of evolution—or, as he preferred to state it, of "descent with modification"—absolutely contradicts Lyell's belief in the fixed nature of species. Each species was constituted at its origin with its definitive characteristics, or so Lyell asserted in defiance of Lamarck when he stated his belief that, in Nature, species have a real existence, and that each of them, at the time of its creation, was endowed with the attributes and the organization by which we distinguish them today. Darwin, who had always maintained friendly relations with Lyell, was very disappointed when he reacted negatively to the publication of *On the Origin of Species by Means of Natural Selection* (1859). In 1866, however, Lyell was forced to concede the point publicly and come around to a certain degree of evolutionism.

Some have regarded this concession as a reluctant retreat in the face of evidence supporting Darwin's theory. What is much more likely is that Lyell was acknowledging that the fossils themselves were giving the lie to his theory. His idea was being called into question by the fact that despite what he had hoped, paleontologists were completely unable to discover traces of mammals in the Paleozoic. Although in 1830 it was still possible to argue that knowledge of these strata was still rudimentary and fragmentary, such was no longer the case thirty years later. Vertebrate paleontology was now revealing a progression and complexity that could no longer be denied.

But however spectacular it may seem, this episode in Charles Lyell's intellectual life must not obscure the way in which his thinking continued to influence Darwin himself and his successors. Although the Latin tag taken up by the author of the *Origin of Species*—"Natura non facit saltum" (Nature makes no leaps)—was first used in the context of natural history by the Swedish scientist Carl von Linné (Linnaeus) (1707–1778), it summarizes the English geologist's philosophy very accurately. Darwin made no secret of the fact that he received from Lyell the idea of gradual evolution, occurring over a very long span of time by the accumulation of small, imperceptible variations.

Darwin thus had to confront the same difficulty that Cuvier had emphasized in refuting Lamarck: the absence of "intermediate forms" in the fossil record, which might have constituted proof of this gradual process. Darwin faced the question unflinchingly, and like Lyell, invoked the lacunary nature of geological data. History would once again play tricks on those who would write it: Darwin's opposition to catastrophism (inspired, as we have just seen, by Lyell) helped establish the notion that his philosophy was similar to Lamarck's. Even today, it is not uncommon to find writers who present Lamarck as the "precursor" of Darwin, despite a vigorous demonstration to the contrary by Madeleine Barthélemy-Madaule in *Lamarck ou la mythe du précurseur*

[Lamarck, or the myth of the precursor]. This is why American (and Soviet) "Darwinism" remained "Lamarckian" for more than a century, producing one of the most fascinating historical misunderstandings in recent memory. It would be comical today if it had not occasionally led to tragedy (no one is likely to forget Lysenko...). The fact is that Darwin had borrowed his gradualism from a scholar who actually never stopped attacking Lamarck, even though—as if deliberately to confuse matters—Lamarck was himself a "gradualist." And Darwin once stated, not without some irritation, that he had "never borrowed a single word or a single idea from Lamarck"!

The fact remains that at the turn of the century, paleontologists were hard at work searching for "intermediate forms," or what were also referred to as "missing links." And some were indeed found, one in particular being *Archaeopteryx*, first found in Germany in 1861: a little vertebrate that looks like a reptile but whose bones were surrounded by the imprints of feathers. However, the very idea of an "intermediate form" led to confusion, as Pascal Tassy expertly demonstrates in the pages which follow. Everyone was looking for "half and half"; but where to stop? Faithful to the gradualism adopted by Darwin and philosophically haunted by the idea of continuity, after each discovery scientists would start asking for another link. Today's American creationists are still eagerly exploiting this logical flaw.

The reader will discover how the rehabilitation of a certain form of discontinuity in the works of Gould and Eldredge (1972)—usually summarized as the "punctuated equilibrium" model—has imbued the message of the fossils with a meaning that frees it from this last ambiguity without by any means calling into question the essence of the theory of natural selection. Although paleontological data do not confirm the neo-Darwinian "synthesis" developed during the 1930s, they do provide "facts" established since then by means of sophisticated dating techniques (carbon-14, which yields dates up to 30,000 years ago, along with potassium–argon, uranium–thorium, etc., which go much further back), in support of the overall viewpoint proposed by the *Origin of Species*.

The philosophical lessons taught in the bright, nimble pages of this little book are far-reaching ones. They force us to confront a radical question: can our imagination really conceive of a history in which what happened—the succession of events of which it consists in our memories—might actually not have happened? Can we accept this simple and powerful idea, particularly the concept that human beings might have appeared only because of a web of circumstances whose necessity can be explained, but whose irreducible contingency must be acknowledged? Darwin himself long hesitated before formulating a thesis so humiliating to our pride. He refused to place humanity at the top of the ladder of beings, as Lamarck had done, or see in it the fruit of a special creation, as Cuvier maintained; but his "materialism" combined with his "continuism" left the door ajar for some naturalized Providence governing the sequence of chance events.... More than one evolutionist has since been engulfed by that opening.

Pascal Tassy begins by discussing the "extraordinary power of the paleontologist" who tells tales of the past; in his closing pages he vividly imparts the pleasure of discovery. But paleontologists today must also endure pain: never turning their gaze, or ours, away from contingency. The message of fossils thus places contemporary thought in an uncomfortable, even painful situation, one that is in any case intolerable to those who seek in Nature an absolute meaning to which they can entrust their existence. This, no doubt, is why paleontology and paleontologists are arousing even livelier passions than ever.

Dominique LECOURT

GEOLOGICAL TIME SCALE

Era	Period	Epoch	Stage	Age* (million years)
Cenozoic	Quaternary	Recent		
		Pleistocene		0.01
	Tertiary	Pliocene		1.65
		Miocene		
		Oligocene		
		Eocene		
		Paleocene		
Mesozoic	Cretaceous	Upper	*Maastrichtian*	65
			Campanian	
			Santonian	
			Coniacian	
		Lower	*Turonian*	
			Cenomanian	
	Jurassic	Upper		135
		Middle		
		Lower		
	Triassic			205
Paleozoic	Permian			245
	Carboniferous	Pennsylvanian		295
		Mississippian		
	Devonian			360
	Silurian			410
	Ordovician			435
	Cambrian			500
Precambrian	Proterozoic			540
	Archaean			2500

AGE OF THE EARTH — 4600

Indicates approximate age at which period or epoch ends

I

TWO CENTURIES

AND THREE

BILLION YEARS

Paleontologists have extraordinary power. Their objects of study—fossils—allow them to tell what has happened on the Earth's surface over time, how life has spread and diversified, which beings disappeared without issue, and which transformed themselves to produce the two million known living species, to which we probably must add some eight million yet to be described.

The history of life is the history of tens of millions of species over more than three billion years. That is why the profession of paleontology excites such lively and contrasting feelings. Paleontologists are fascinating because they can tell a tale that touches all our genealogical fantasies. They are also troubling, or at least they have caused considerable trouble, because that tale was believed to have been written down already in the revealed Books: consultation of the archives of the planet was considered blasphemy.

The power of the paleontologist is as great as his or her audacity: reconstructions are based on nothing more than imprints, fragments, shells, carapaces, bones, and teeth. What are fossils, after all, if not vestiges both destroyed and preserved by time? The task of paleontology is to decipher, laboriously and meticulously, these vestiges. Everyone knows the boast of Georges Cuvier (1769–1832), founder of the discipline: from a single bone, even a portion of a bone, the anatomist can reconstruct an entire animal.

Although for more than two centuries paleontologists have been contributing, day after day, new pieces to the puzzle of life on Earth, their virtuosity is still amazing. But our amazement is still tinged with suspicion: Where do paleontologists gain their knowledge? What is the basis for their legitimacy? Don't they say more than they should? Should we believe them when they tell us all about the rhythm of evolution in living beings based on a few shells? Don't paleontologists contradict themselves, and often? And what about all the theories, even diametrically opposed ones, coming one on the heels of the last? But fascination always wins out over suspicion: who could turn away from the landscapes, the flora and fauna developing on this Earth over hundreds of millions of years? Who could remain unmoved by a description of the first forms of life on our planet? And who could fail to wonder about the appearance and the lives of our close (and not so close) ancestors?

PETRIFIED TIME

A fossil is "petrified time," to use the lovely image of Georges Canguilhem. To act as the depository of time is a rare privilege, and the chronological dimension of a fossil thus gives it a very particular epistemological status. An object out of the past, imprisoned in geological strata, is a direct eyewitness to history. Very few 20th-century paleontologists do not believe that it represents a *real* proof of evolution. The creationists saw the problem very clearly: never mind the discoveries of the embryologists and geneticists, the identity between early embryonic phases in humans, cows, and fish, the discovery of the double helix of DNA, and mutations in fruit flies: it was *fossils* that had to be discredited. Enormous publicity was therefore heaped on the few fakes that have disgraced the history of paleontology. But those fakes are extremely rare: everyone mentions Piltdown Man because there is not much else to mention! Piltdown Man was cobbled together in 1912 from a human cranium and the jawbone of an ape that some clever and malicious hand (the identity of whose owner is still a mystery) had carefully touched up so that its characteristics looked a little less simian. The hoax was a masterful one, and the fact that paleontologists allowed themselves to be taken in by it does little for the prestige of the profession (not everyone was fooled, but that seldom-made statement is certainly no excuse).

Today another affair may provide fuel for a similar outburst of sarcasm. A considerable amount of work on the fauna of the Himalayas may need to be purely and simply dumped out the window. For many years, an Indian paleontologist claimed to be finding fossils in a number of sites discovered on his expeditions. The results were all published in collaboration with international experts. Now, however, it turns out that these fossils—an ammonite here, a fish there—came from everywhere *but* the Himalayas! The hoax was uncovered by an Australian paleontologist: this time it was not the fossils that were fakes, but their identity as *Himalayan* fossils. Nevertheless, this kind of trickery is extremely rare, very simply because no one would derive any advantage from fabricating, say, a fossil sea-urchin, even if it did change some evolutionary hypothesis: it would affect too few people, and the media effect would be zero. Making a big publicity splash requires spectacular fossils which cry out to the imagination: in this case the task is extremely difficult, and in fact almost impossible.

Among the first paleontologists in the 19th century, opinion as to the message of fossils was split. Some (and not the least among them) did not consider fossils to be proofs of evolution. Ever since the origins of paleontological science, the fossil, eyewitness to the Earth's history, has been called upon to tell different stories—stories in which perhaps evolution played no part, and even stories in which, to the contrary, the fossil was believed to demonstrate the futility of the transformist theory. The fossil thus has an ambiguous epistemological status: it embodies a history, but only the paleontologist can tell that history, and must take the risk of interpreting it in the light of his or her own culture, religious preoccupations, assumptions, analytical methods, and models.

We know that Leonardo da Vinci (1452–1519) and Bernard Palissy (1510–1589) recognized the antiquity of shells and other fossil remains referred to as glossopetra. In 1715, René-Antoine de Réaumur (1683–1757) related, in a famous treatise, that since the 17th century a small local industry had been extracting "turquoise" from the ground in the Gers region of southwestern France. Certain stones, often bluish or yellowish, were heated in a furnace to give them the blue-green tinge of turquoise. These stones resembled bones or teeth. Réaumur stated that "the materials which supply our turquoise are petrified bones," and that some of them "are no less visibly teeth than the glossopetra." He illustrated some "turquoise" stones that can easily be identified: they are indeed the remains of the bones and teeth of Tertiary mammals.

But a famous contemporary of Réaumur, none other than Voltaire (1694–1778), poked fun at the supposed fossils reported from the Alps, the shells that some believed to be eyewitnesses to vanished worlds: no, sneered the philosopher, they were quite simply shells left there by pilgrims on their way to Saint James of Compostela in Spain. Nothing would seem more contrary to good sense, after all, than to regard mountains as piles composed largely of sediments deposited by the sea.

On the eve of the French Revolution, Georges-Louis Leclerc, Comte de Buffon (1707–1788), who already believed that the time span of Creation greatly exceeded that indicated by Genesis, had conceded that certain large molars and bones the size of those of elephants, collected in North America and Russia, belonged to vanished species. One molar from Russia ("Little Tartary"), a drawing of which he published in 1778, proved decades later to belong to a distant cousin of the elephants to which the name *Mastodon borsoni* was given in 1834.

Could all these fossil remnants be regarded as evidence of *the* Flood? Many naturalists believed just that; it was what Cuvier supposed, with some modifications. There is no question that the founder of vertebrate paleontology in France was a constant opponent of the evolutionist ideas being defended at that same time by Jean-Baptiste de Monet, Chevalier de Lamarck (1744–1829). Immortalized in history as the architect of the doctrine of "transformism," although he himself never used the term and it appeared only later on, Lamarck can also be regarded as the founder of invertebrate paleontology. From 1802 to 1806 he published a series of monographs on the fossil invertebrates of the Paris basin, which remained valuable reference works for many years. By taking this approach, Lamarck became an expert analyst of variation, and he concluded that species exhibited continuity over time. Cuvier, on the other hand, advanced the notion of "lost species." Too perceptive an anatomist not to seize upon everything that differentiated among the fossil vertebrates that he studied with such zeal, he developed a theory of "revolutions on the surface of the globe": in other words, catastrophism. According to Cuvier, catastrophes had repeatedly eradicated living beings from the planet. Each time, following these repeated deluges, Creation took up where it had left off, improving its productions as necessary. It is true that the morphology of the shells studied by Lamarck was not fundamentally different from that of present-day shells. It is also true that Cuvier analyzed anatomies with no modern equivalent, and that none of the fossil vertebrates that he described could be regarded as the direct ancestor of present-day species. Still, the "organizational plan" of the fossil mammals studied by Cuvier was very obviously the same as that of living mammals. The similarity went no further, or so said Cuvier.

The organization of the giant South American sloth, the *Megatherium* described by Cuvier, was definitely that of a mammal. It resembled the modern sloth, a small, arboreal, and very shy animal. But because of numerous characteristics, *Megatherium* could not have been its direct ancestor. The famous *Paleotherium* of the Montmartre gypsum had undeniable affinities with living ungulate herbivorous mammals, especially with horses and tapirs. But nothing in present-day Nature was very similar to *Paleotherium*. Cuvier therefore saw in these fossil vertebrates a decisive argument against the concept of evolution.

For both Lamarck and Cuvier, and later for Charles Darwin (1809–1882), the idea of evolution became associated with that of the transformation of species. Only a direct connection between a fossil species and a living one could actualize it: once such a connection had been demonstrated, the theory of evolution was proven. In a way, Cuvier was not entirely wrong when he concluded, from observing his fossils, that this direct connection was absent. Undoubtedly if he had simply replaced the notion of direct descent with that of shared ancestry, he would have looked at the world differently. But the idea of a fossil and a living being sharing an ancestor involves an additional entity: another fossil, the actual common ancestor, a fossil that one is not actually looking at. This entity then becomes a hypothesis rather than an observed fact, and Cuvier wanted to stick to the observed facts. This would later be seen as an epistemological weakness, as "strict empiricism," but it must also be understood as the price of his unequaled talent as an anatomist. Cuvier had very quickly observed the presence of unique features in his fossils, and each feature helped rub out the "fact" of evolution.

But as descriptions of fossil species (especially invertebrates) continued to accumulate, the connections among fossils on the one hand, and between fossils and living organisms on the other hand, became closer and closer. Cuvier's successive floods threatened to become perpetual motion, and catastrophism gradually lost its credibility. But the paleontologists in Cuvier's tradition somehow maintained that tradition against all opposition. Alcide d'Orbigny (1802–1857), whom some depict as the founder of biostratigraphy (the study of the succession of fauna in geological strata), postulated twenty-eight reiterated Creations, in which the reproduction of often very similar fauna, differing only in terms of minor transformations, does seem to indicate considerable persistence on the part of the Creator.

On the other hand, the ideas which characterized Lamarck's evolutionism—the continuity of life and the "creative" power of time—gradually won adherents among naturalists. One of them, Frédéric Gérard, a forgotten popularizer of Lamarck's ideas, even coined the expression "theory of the evolution of organized beings," in its modern sense, in 1845. Although Gérard was editor in chief of the *Dictionnaire universel d'histoire naturelle* [Universal dictionary of natural history] supervised by the geologist Charles d'Orbigny (1806–1876)—brother of Alcide—history has not been kind to his memory. Goulven Laurent, the historian of science, informs us that even the dates of his birth and death are unknown. One of the perpetuators of Lamarck's work, the anatomist Étienne Geoffroy Saint-Hilaire (1772–1844), gives evidence of a different perception of fossil vertebrates from the one championed by Cuvier. Having completed, in 1831, a study of fossil crocodiles from the Jurassic in Normandy, he concluded that there was a continuous link, with transformation, between the fossil and living species: "The animals living today derive [...] from the animals of the antediluvian world," he wrote without the slightest ambiguity. By doing so, he was putting into practice a research program that he had first formulated in 1807: the task of the evolutionists was to "show how [living species] could be related, by a sort of descent, to those of the first inhabitants of the Earth, a knowledge of which is transmitted to us by their remains in the fossil state."

Of course it was with Darwin and the *Origin of Species*, first published in 1859, that the theory of evolution began to prevail. Darwin's theory differed from Lamarck's not in the idea that evolution was a reality (a concept already completely accepted by Lamarck), but above all because it postulated a single history, and proposed a mechanism to explain the fact of evolution: natural selection of variations. We are interested here, however, only in the place of fossils in this theory. Darwin was evidently disturbed by the ambivalence of fossils, used by the founders of paleontology alternately to prove and refute the concept of evolution. It is worth remembering that in his *Philosophie zoologique* of 1809—the first work to present a doctrine of evolution—Lamarck himself made almost no use of fossils. It is tempting to explain this paradox, revived by Darwin, by once again invoking the multitude of living forms (or "taxonomic diversity," in scientific language). Although it was becoming denser every year, the fossil record still exhibited enormous gaps.

These gaps are easily explained if one considers the sheer scale of geologic time: more than three billion years of biological evolution! Surely it is unreasonable to ask that the entire continuity of this phenomenon be revealed to us. I should add that fossilization is a random phenomenon: the preservation of the remains of living beings—even the hard parts—appears to be the exception. The deposits of ancient seas, lakes, and rivers that produce fossils in fact only rarely preserve them. Decomposition, alteration, erosion, abrasion, and chemical dissolution remain the rule. Geologic history makes the task even more complicated: ancient sediments are accessible to us only because they happen to be at the surface, in other words because of certain tectonic and sedimentary events that have affected the planet. We therefore find that fossil-bearing deposits are simply the result of combinations of geological happenstance, so that for certain epochs in which they are rare, they provide fauna that appear entirely new, segments of diversity that literally irrupt into the fossil record.

In Darwin's eyes fossils did not show, in detail, this image of progressive and gradual evolution that would have agreed with his own notions. He was therefore inclined to emphasize the gaps in the fossil record more than the information it provided. But these gaps in no way contradicted the theory of evolution. According to Darwin, fossils supported his theory by illustrating, on a grand scale, the progressive transformation of the living world; the trouble was, they did not provide all the information needed to understand the mechanisms that must have been at work in the genesis of species. With Darwinism, the ambiguity of the fossil message came to an end: invoking repeated Creations for each species revealed by the paleontologists became literally absurd. Even if the information that they transmitted was not sufficient to answer every question about the mechanisms governing the origin of species, fossils—representing "snapshots" of the gigantic process represented by geologic time—became one of the pillars of the theory of evolution.

The biologists who ensured that Darwin's ideas triumphed, such as Ernst Haeckel (1834–1919), saw in fossils one of the sources of evolutionary science. That science was based on comparative anatomy, ontogeny (the study of development), and paleontology (the study of fossils): these are the three major disciplines of systematics, the science of the diversity of living beings over time and space. Genetics came later, and with it the end of the harmonious egalitarianism among the evolutionary sciences.

A VERY OLD STORY

Fossils thus became one of the major proofs of evolution. The first genealogy associating modern and fossil species in their stratigraphic context was prepared, in 1866, by the French paleontologist Albert Gaudry (1827–1908), also a great discoverer of fossil vertebrates in Greece.

Today it is easy to trace the broad outlines of the evolution of life based exclusively on fossil documents. Despite its random aspects, fossilization turns out to be sufficiently frequent to yield a coherent story. One could look at the progress of life as an increasing diversification and complexification of living beings, caused by the inheritance of millions and millions of years of various transformations. For my part, I do not regard this evolutionary unfolding as "progress," if progress is to be understood as replacement of primitive beings by evolved beings. This widely-held notion of evolutionary links smacks of anthropocentrism. Numerous beings considered primitive as measured against *Homo sapiens* have never been replaced by more evolved beings. The very idea of an evolved species is a completely relative one, and basically does not correspond to any general criterion. Can we say that *Diplodocus* was less evolved than a common lizard simply because it has disappeared? Is a bat, which has developed a sonar system so it can fly and hunt, really less evolved than an *Australopithecus* which walks upright on two legs? What about bacteria? They have been diversifying since the origins of life and are now so ubiquitous that we cannot figure out how to get rid of them: don't they represent a stunning example of evolutionary success? Many lines that emerged hundreds of millions of years ago are still present. Every living species bears witness to successive branchings which constructed, over time, the evolutionary tree. Fossils both embody this history and inform us about branches that are entirely extinct.

Fossils can be utilized for many other experiments; there is more to them than just observing, analyzing, and classifying their shapes. Fossilized bones sometimes preserve proteins. Tens of millions of years old, these substances can still produce immunological reactions, which can be used to compare fossil species to living species. For example, the collagen in fossil bones retains a number of its properties. One is the ability to indicate, upon examination of its carbon and nitrogen isotopes (chemical elements that differ from one another only in terms of atomic weight), the proportion of animal or plant food in an organism's diet. From this alone, we can deduce how extinct animals lived—as carnivores or herbivores—and one can even distinguish between grazers and leaf-eaters. It then becomes possible to reconstruct the paleoenvironment of these fossils. Along the same investigative lines, it may be possible to reconstruct ancient climates by analyzing oxygen isotopes in the shells of fossil foraminifera (single-celled marine animals). Oxygen isotope ratios vary depending on whether the water is warm or cold, and are even different in ice and snow. The shells reflect isotopic changes in sea water, and this has allowed researchers to establish an accurate scale of paleoclimatic changes over time. Today it is also possible to analyze the microstructure of fossils and understand certain biological mineralization phenomena. In addition, the scratches and other abrasion traces on the enamel of a mammalian tooth can be examined under the scanning electron microscope to determine what kind of diet its owner was eating. Some workers are also analyzing the traces left on certain bones by pathological factors, which can be used to trace the individual history of the organism to whom the bones belonged, and sometimes to identify hereditary diseases.

But it is the history of life on Earth, now outlined with the help of fossils, that is still the most fascinating subject for everyone. It can be read like a novel, but it is not fiction. Fossils can be used to accurately locate the great events in evolution. They always yield a minimum age: the first known fossils belonging to a given group are not necessarily the organisms that are actually the oldest ones; very often, later paleontological discoveries will push back the origin of a group.

The first known sedimentary rocks (the Isha formation in Greenland, 3.7 billion years old) seem to have yielded the first traces of life. The first structures resulting from the activity of living beings are only slightly younger (3.5 billion years). These are the stromatolites, discovered in southern Africa (Swaziland and Zambia): stacks of limestone produced by the action of single-celled microorganisms with no nuclei (bacteria and *Cyanophyceae*, also called blue-green algae). Similar structures can still be observed today being formed in intertidal zones in the warm seas of the Bahamas and Australia. As for the first bacterium, it was discovered in the Precambrian of southern Africa (Zimbabwe), and is 3.2 billion years old.

The first organisms containing chlorophyll have been dated to 2 billion years ago. They played a considerable role in the history of our planet: in the process of photosynthesis, these organisms released oxygen into the atmosphere and into ocean waters. Very quickly—in geological terms, of course—starting 1.5 billion years ago, the first nucleated cells ("eukaryotes") appeared. The eukaryotes diversified into multicellular beings at the very end of the Precambrian, especially at Ediacara in Australia (670 million years ago), but also in Europe and North America. Here we find the first impressions of jellyfish and soft corals (animals belonging to the coelenterate lineage), worms, perhaps some arthropods without exoskeletons, and groups of uncertain affinity: lineages that left no descendants, all of them soft-bodied animals. Some impressions, however, might be nothing more than bacterial films which were deposited on the mud and then were deformed.

Starting with the Cambrian period, a hundred million years later, we find the first remains of animals with hard parts, in other words an external skeleton such as a carapace or shell. This is the case with the fauna of the Burgess Shale in Canada, also recently discovered in China. It contains sponges, algae, and brachiopods. Arthropods are very numerous in it, especially the fossil group of the trilobites (so called because their bodies are divided length-wise into three parts). One soft-bodied arthropod, *Naraoia*, is noteworthy because it is unquestionably related to the trilobites, but has certain very specific anatomical features. It bears witness to an already very extensive history of which so far we have discovered no trace. The Burgess fauna also contains echinoderms (a phylum resembling starfish, holothuria, and sea urchins), and various groups of worms. Finally, and most importantly, twenty or so of the species discovered at the Burgess site cannot be assigned to groups that presently exist: they each correspond to a lineage that had already differentiated and would later expand, exceptional evidence for a diversification whose initial stages are still hidden from us. Lastly, *Pikaia*, a little worm-like animal, is probably related to the chordates (animals with a dorsal cord), in other words to the animals belonging to the great phylum that includes the vertebrates. In total, this fauna reflects the first great taxonomic explosion in the fossil archives, some 600 million years ago.

The first traces of an internal skeleton—the remains of vertebrates—date back 500 million years; all of them are from marine environments.

The Ordovician (ca. 450 million years ago) produced the first complete skeletons belonging to vertebrates (*Sacabambaspis janvieri* from Bolivia). These were animals without paired fins, living in a marine environment. Fossil spores indicate that mosses had already conquered the dry land.

In the Devonian, between 410 and 360 million years ago, we see an explosion of aquatic vertebrates into lake and river environments on the northern continents, which at that time were united. At the same epoch, terrestrial insects and vascular plants were diversifying; the first ferns appeared. At the very end of the Devonian, following the lead of the collembolan insects, the arachnids, and the millipedes, vertebrates began their conquest of the continents. The amphibian *Ichthyostega* discovered in Greenland is the best known of the first tetrapods, but others have been found in Russia and Australia. "Seed ferns" appear in this epoch, and would give rise to all the seed-bearing plants known today.

In the Carboniferous, 300 million years ago, immense forests of tree ferns and giant horsetails stretched over the Earth. The air echoed to the buzz of dragonflies with wingspans of almost three feet. Giant millipedes up to ten feet long crawled below. The rivers, lakes, and marshes were filled with amphibians. Other tetrapods, at first glance little different from the amphibians, would have a bright future. These animals—the first of the amniotes—laid very special eggs in which the embryo was protected by new coatings. As a result, reproduction no longer depended exclusively on an aquatic environment. The fossilized eggs that have been discovered so far are much later in date, but Carboniferous amniotes can be distinguished from modern amphibians by certain skeletal characteristics. The major groups of amniotes diversified very quickly during the Carboniferous: the lineage that would produce mammals is represented by a group called pelycosaurs, which at this point have nothing mammalian about them except the morphology of the temporal fossa. The line that would lead to modern lizards, crocodiles, and birds can also be identified a little later, with the *Petrolacosaurus* of North America.

The first mammals in the strict sense lived 200 million years ago, along with the first Diptera (flies and mosquitoes): they were small shrew-like animals with none of the distinguishing characteristics of the various major groups of mammals extant today. The first live-bearing mammals, related to present-day marsupials and placental mammals, are 110 million years old.

The first known bird is 140 million years old: *Archaeopteryx* of the Upper Jurassic in Germany, an animal that had feathers but also claws and teeth. The only known Jurassic bird, it now has successors in two fossils that are 10–20 million years younger (Lower Cretaceous), and a little bit more evolved; these were only recently discovered, one in Spain and the other in China. The Hymenoptera (bees and wasps) and Coleoptera (beetles) were already

present at this epoch; a little later (Lower Cretaceous) came the Lepidoptera (butterflies).

Eighty million years ago (Upper Cretaceous)
we see a diversification of the first plants with flow-
ers and fruit. Landscapes began to resemble what we
are familiar with today, except for those shaped by
human activity. This activity becomes evident first of
all from the first manufactured tools, probably associated with intelligence: they are 2.7 million years
old, from Ethiopia. The first deliberate burials are
100,000 years old, and the first artistic manifesta-
tions, illustrated by the wall paintings in the cave at
Lascaux, appear approximately 20,000 years ago.

There is nothing conjectural about this story. It
represents the current status of scientific knowledge
and dating concerning the history of life. One of the
most important goals of the first paleontologists was
also to construct a chronological scale of geologic
time. This time scale, based on fossil successions and
fossil evolution, and on estimates of sedimentation
rate, showed very quickly that the period of Creation
set down in Genesis was infinitely too short to
account for the history of life. This scale has since
undergone revisions, but they have always been cor-
rections and refinements, never revolutions. Later
on, so-called "absolute" radiometric dates, based on
measurements of the natural radioactivity in rocks,
have confirmed and refined the "relative" dates
deduced by stratigraphers, which in turn were based

on the succession of geological strata. Certain kinds of contamination, either natural or resulting from handling, will occasionally falsify radiometric data (carbon-14, potassium–argon, etc.), but as a general rule, absolute dates—independent of any conjectures concerning evolutionary pace or sedimentation rates—have confirmed beyond a shadow of a doubt both the antiquity of life on Earth, and the dates of the major phases of organic evolution.

The chapters in the story whose broad outlines I have just related are marked by fossils. Some have only been discovered very recently, and many still remain to be found. They give us information not only about vertical linkages but also about horizontal relationships: in other words, geographical distribution. Fossils of terrestrial vertebrates—and also those of plants, which have little ability to disperse—tell us about relationships among the continents themselves. When the German meteorologist Alfred Wegener (1880–1930) developed the theory of "continental drift," the evidence that he used included the distribution of fossils.

Some examples have taken on almost mythological stature in the history of paleontology and biogeography: one is *Mesosaurus*, a small freshwater amniote of the Permian (Upper Paleozoic), traces of which have been found only in southern Africa and in South America. This southerly distribution of animals which, to all appearances, would have been unable to migrate across oceans, was interpreted as evidence for the former existence of a single geographical province common to the two continents that are now separated, at a time when the Atlantic Ocean did not exist. This agglomeration was called Gondwanaland, from the name of a region in India. Since then, the discovery of fossils between the Permian and the base of the Tertiary has reinforced the idea that a single continental mass, Pangaea, had fragmented into two great blocks, Laurasia (from *Laurentia* for North American and *Asia*) to the north and Gondwanaland to the south; the latter then became subdivided in turn as the Atlantic opened up.

The discovery of terrestrial vertebrates in Antarctica, beginning in the late 1960s, made a considerable splash. The fossils in question were those of animals from the late Permian (250 million years ago), "mammalian reptiles" known from Africa, India, and South America which therefore belonged to Gondwanaland. In 1991, the description of a dinosaur from Antarctica, by the British paleontologist J. J. Hooker and his co-workers, confirmed once again the existence of this supercontinent and the ancient connections between Antarctica and South America. In the meantime, geophysical data had given new life to Wegener's theory. The indirect arguments have now become direct: today we can use satellites and space stations to measure the rate at which Europe is moving away from North America. The fossil documentation had foreshadowed these results, demonstrating that the present-day continents had not always been in their current positions, even though paleontologists and geologists had for a long time refused to see the implications.

II

FOSSILS

AND EVOLUTION

Considering the evolutionary scenario proposed in the previous chapter, one might believe that the history of life can be read directly from the rocks. Of course that is by no means the case. Deciphering evolution by examining fossils means using a theoretical "filter." But at every turn, paleontologists themselves have willingly given the impression that their analyses were based not on speculation, but on an "objective" reconstruction of past reality. The source of this belief is obviously the ambiguous status of fossils.

FACTS AND THEORIES

Every evolutionist after Darwin has always considered fossils to be tangible proof of evolution. Obviously in order to *see* what our ancestors—and those of every other species living today—were made of, one merely needs to consult the fossils. A fossil is a "fact" simply because it is an object, and an object whose real existence cannot reasonably be called into question. But as we have already seen,

53

this object possesses a very defining dimension: the dimension of time, which gives a fossil its particular status. What we see is more than a fragment, a shell, a bone, or an imprint of a vanished being: we are looking at a piece of history.

Oddly enough, thanks to fossils, no one can dispute the fact that a unique history of life has unfolded over more than three billion years; but the great question remains: Which history? The genealogical tree offers an answer by narrating the story. But it can happen that using the same objects, the same fossils, two paleontologists, each as competent as the other, can construct two different genealogical trees and tell two different stories. Sometimes the textbooks present incompatible evolutions, and schools clash: what is truth in Stockholm and Paris is error in London and Chicago. This dualism is intolerable: there cannot be two histories of life. Of course a fossil is a fact, but as soon as it is interpreted, as soon as it becomes intelligible, it acquires a cargo of theory and thus becomes a scientific object, and by that very fact becomes conjectural and subject to dispute.

A careful reading of the paleontological literature reveals a ferment of improvements, retouching, and reworking, but also radical transformations in the interpretation of the facts. These changes over the decades can be explained first of all by discoveries. Each new fossil explains a little more history, and by doing so forces a tiny change in the history that had previously been reconstructed. Evolution is contingent, and each discovery could potentially be a source of correction. Most importantly, hypotheses about genealogical connections end up changing the previously acknowledged historical scenarios, sometimes quite radically. Such is the task of phylogenetic research (from *phylum*, group or race), the study of the appearance or genesis of related groups of organisms: to infer hypotheses concerning relationships among fossil lineages, and consequently among extant ones. It is easy to achieve consensus on the identification of objects; otherwise the paleontological literature would be pure cacophony, and paleontology simply would not exist. It is more difficult to reach agreement about hypotheses concerning evolutionary links between fossils. Contradictory inferences about phylogenetic relationships among fossil species or groups of species will inevitably arise from different scenarios. What is more, the theoretical filter that is used to analyze the fossils can also influence the result, and not only with regard to the phylogenetic reconstruction of a given group. This is exactly what has happened with the fundamental debate, beginning almost twenty years ago, about the tempo of evolution.

Evolutionary reconstructions devised by paleontologists do not draw their objectivity from an assertion that they are based on incontestable "facts" (i.e., fossils). The time is long past when paleontologists, such as Georges Depéret (1854–1929) at the beginning of this century, could invoke fossils as the only *real* facts pertinent to evolutionary theory. Paleontological constructions partake of objective knowledge only if they can be tested and checked— in a word, if they can be refuted. When it comes to historical science, however, the idea of testing becomes a source of dispute. This is why paleontology is still sometimes considered a "subjective science," a singularly pejorative term for a discipline trying to claim some universality. Nevertheless, it is possible to assess and evaluate: not all histories are equal, and some are more probable than others. Testing them involves more than just the discovery of new fossils, otherwise the foundations of paleontological hypotheses would be very poorly developed. But however self-evident this observation might be, the importance of new discoveries cannot be underestimated. There are still considerable gaps in the fossil record: even today, we understand only fragments of the history of life. True, the fragments are considerable, and already the history of life on Earth is intelligible to us. But an infinity of fossils remains to be discovered.

Testing phylogenetic hypotheses, and choosing among different evolutionary scenarios developed from the same observations, basically involves cultivating a prejudice for simplicity. The arrangements of fossils with respect to one another can be used to reconstruct various more or less significant segments of the genealogical tree. These segments represent the phylogeny of groups. The genus *Dyospira*, the hominids, the actinopterygians or the hyaenids, the trilobites or *Choerolophodon*, *Hyopsodus* or the theridomyids—all constitute such groups, with names that will be variously evocative or obscure depending on the reader's familiarity with botany, zoology, or paleontology. Many phylogenetic hypotheses advanced since the 19th century have still never been refuted following discoveries of new fossils or new characteristics (including genetic information in cases where extant species are involved): they appear to be so solid that they are now regarded as observed facts. Yet they remain reconstructions in which formal reasoning has its place. Phylogenies do not simply reveal themselves to the trained eye of the paleontologist during field surveys: they need to be reconstructed using criteria which implicitly embody the idea of simplicity.

Similarity and stratigraphic superposition are the criteria most often cited in support of historical reconstructions in paleontology. Here the principle of simplicity applies to the interpretation of the similarity: it is only when two fossils are similar to one another that it is simpler to postulate an exclusive link. In general terms, this simplicity criterion is based on the principle of "economy of hypotheses," also called the "parsimony principle" (a term from molecular taxonomy applied in this case to evolutionary hypotheses). Beginning with a given number of observations drawn both from fossils and from modern organisms, one attempts to construct, for the particular species or groups of species being studied, an arrangement which involves a minimum of evolutionary events. A solution that implies the least number of events cannot be less probable than a solution that implies more. This principle is a stringent method of selecting among competing hypotheses, scenarios, and histories. Only those systematics specialists called "cladists" refer explicitly to this principle. The phylogenetic construction methods developed under the rubric of "phylogenetic systematics" by the German entomologist Willi Hennig (1913–1976) are now subsumed into a discipline called "cladism." The term comes from "clade," the name given in the technical jargon of systematics to natural groups, in other words groups that comprise species which share the same genealogical history. In the modern epoch, for example, birds and crocodiles belong to a natural group, since they are the only descendants of a far-off ancestral species that lived in the Mesozoic era. This group does not appear in the neo-Darwinian manuals, however, which classify crocodiles as reptiles along with lizards and turtles.

Does this principle of economy meet a simple methodological need, or is it, on the contrary, based on the ontology of living species? I have addressed these topics of phylogenetic construction elsewhere, and I will not come back to them here. I do, however, feel the need to emphasize that hypotheses about links among fossil (and living) species are logical constructs. Starting with the postulate that the power of evolution is unlimited, one might state, for example, that anything is possible: any fossil species might have given rise to any other one; any group could be related to any other one. This approach quickly leads nowhere. The only alternative, however, lies between this option (anything might have happened) and the logic that dictates the inevitability of simplicity.

But there is a very real phenomenon which complicates the situation: it is convergence—the independent appearance of identical characteristics in different species, whether genealogically close or distant. This phenomenon implies that similar evolutionary events can be repeated, whereas the fact that different species share a single characteristic inherited from a common ancestral species implies only a single evolutionary event. There has always been a great temptation to place too much emphasis on convergence, since it is easily perceptible when comparing living forms, and becomes historically concrete when one studies fossils.

A simple (and oft-cited) example will illustrate the problem. Terrestrial vertebrates (tetrapods) are descended from a bony fish with lobed fins, of a rather specific type. The "emergence from the sea" happened in the Devonian, some 380 million years ago, the era of the first tetrapods. All tetrapods, both fossil and living, share a single basic anatomy, if only in terms of limb structure. Postulating a single evolutionary event to explain the appearance of the tetrapods means acknowledging that they have a single origin, and therefore recognizing that all tetrapods are descended from a single ancestral species (this is called the monophyletic hypothesis). The opposite has of course been proposed: perhaps several aquatic species evolved in parallel, yielding the same structures each time (the polyphyletic hypothesis). Considering the particular characteristics involved, the polyphyletic hypothesis turns out to be less economical, and would therefore be rejected.

But when we consider the magnitude of time and the depth of the geological strata, the logic of genealogical analysis really seems less clear-cut. Is it not true that the sedimentary layers offer us only a fragment of history? Once again, we are observing the products of evolution, and not the links that might have existed between them. One way to sidestep the dilemma and transcend all speculation is to take an extreme "positivist" approach, limiting oneself to situations in which the sedimentary gaps appear negligible, and the fossil record is sufficiently complete for the older fossils to be regarded as the direct ancestors of recent ones. It is then possible almost to "read" the direction of evolution in the rocks. I must emphasize again that direct relationships among fossils cannot be constructed without analyzing their similarities: a Devonian amphibian is not the ancestor of a Carboniferous dragonfly. From this ludicrous example comes the rule that what is older cannot automatically be considered the ancestor of what is more recent. This also applies to morphologically similar species. But similarity is not a given: it is the result of interpretation. Nothing is less intuitive than a resemblance resulting from descent. The special cases that I have just mentioned are cited in order to illustrate the solidity of paleontological constructs, specifically those in which hypotheses are thought to play only a small part. However, later discoveries often demonstrate how rash it is to assume that a fossil record is complete!

"Cladistic" analysis of characteristics, which aims at defining the simplest genealogical solution, has become a widely used paleontological tool over the last twenty years. In fact it is now possible to date paleontological publications by looking at the structure of the genealogical trees used to illustrate them! At the outset, the cladists were nothing if not aggressive; I will never forget the spectacular arguments, even heated exchanges, that enlivened certain highly polarized scientific conferences. By demolishing a number of unnecessarily complex learned scenarios that had in some cases become gospel, the cladists sowed discord in the ranks of evolutionists. The reader need not worry: the "simple" solutions offered by the cladists are still complicated enough to preserve the appearance of science. But it is obvious that cladism, by placing preponderant emphasis (with an enthusiasm that is often felt to be heavy-handed) on the logic inherent in genealogical constructs, has had an impact on more than one naturalist.

THE TEMPO OF EVOLUTION

There would be very little point in taking time to compare the contradictory phylogenies of various fossils, using the simplicity filter (or the parsimony model, if you prefer) to select those that seem the most probable. But above and beyond historical construction, the message of the fossils deals with evolutionary mechanisms that never fail to arouse interest (and with good reason). The most instructive approach to this question would therefore be to look at the debate about evolutionary tempos and modes as revealed to us by fossils. *Tempo and Mode in Evolution* was in fact the title of the book by the American paleontologist George Gaylord Simpson (1902–1984) that first appeared in 1944 and influenced many evolutionists who learned the fundamentals of their discipline in the immediate postwar period. In this pioneering work, Simpson first asks a question: "How fast, as a matter of fact, do animals evolve in Nature? That is the fundamental observational problem of tempo in evolution." The problem is just as important today, as are the two classes of solution to it discussed at that time by Simpson: gradual or "phyletic" evolution, and rapid or "quantum" evolution. Nor have Simpson's explorations of the concepts of micro-, macro-, and megaevolution lost any of their relevance, except that the term "megaevolution," referring to evolution on a large scale (family, order, class, and phylum), is now no longer used. But there is still a very lively debate concerning microevolution (intraspecific evolution, taking place within the species) and macroevolution (interspecific evolution, taking place between species, "at or near the minimum level of genetic discontinuity," as Simpson puts it).

This liveliness is evident in the debate between the phyletic gradualism model and the model of "punctuated equilibrium" that describes quantum evolution. For twenty years this debate has excited controversy and dispute, some of it virulent. Is evolution slow and gradual, or rapid and jerky? In 1972, when the American paleontologists Niles Eldredge and Stephen Jay Gould proposed their model for speciation (the formation of species) referred to as "punctuated equilibrium," they were deliberately throwing a wrench into conventional paleontological thinking. Until then, despite the distinctions established by Simpson, most paleontological publications adhered to the "gradualist" model, and conformed to the idea of phyletic evolution. According to the model that can be called dominant, a study of fossil series showed that phyletic lineages changed gradually over time; if discontinuities appeared between the segments of that lineage, they were attributed to gaps in the stratigraphic documentation. Such was the neo-Darwinian orthodoxy in paleontology. Eldredge and Gould took issue with this, stating that far from never making leaps, Nature in fact proceeded in phases of stability ("stasis" is actually the canonical term) and phases of rapid transformation: the periods of stability, or equilibrium, were "punctuated" by periods of intense evolution that were the fountainhead of speciation.

Previously, most attention had been focused on cases of phyletic gradualism, many instances of which have appeared in the paleontological literature since the end of the 19th century. In a way, these examples do show the progressive transformation of one species into another over time. What more could one ask for as proof of the reality of Darwinian evolution?

Whether the species are plankton, oysters, sea urchins, ammonites, or rodents, there are plentiful examples. The initial model is relatively simple: in a given basin, superposition in the stratigraphic layers of fossils belonging to a lineage allows one to "see" the direction of evolution. The observed characteristics (which often include size) are quantified. Transformations indicate a progressive morphological drift, along with occasional backtracking. The most recent members of the lineage are different from the oldest ones, the ends seamlessly linked by intermediate forms. But some of these "classic" examples, on which generations of students cut their paleontological teeth, were found to be in error long before 1972. One concerns the gradual evolution of a fossil sea urchin, *Micraster*, a typical gradualist example dating back to 1899. It has now been demonstrated, however, that the progressive transformation, *in situ* in a sedimentary basin, from one species of *Micraster* to another was an artifact. The recent species was a migrant from another basin— but it took sixty years to set the story straight, sixty years of triumphant gradualism. I do not want to give the impression that every example of phyletic gradualism ever advanced is erroneous, but there are not as many genuine cases as the paleontological literature would lead one to believe. Some instances show nothing but a sort of zigzag, fluctuating variation with no clear orientation, allowing different paleontologists to see them as examples either of gradual evolution or of stasis, "non-evolution." One contemporary French paleontologist, Jean Chaline, has presented examples of gradualism (including the evolution of the first lower molar in Eurasian field mice over 3.5 million years), but even he does not hesitate to admit that well-documented, well-researched examples of irreversible gradual evolution "are, in the final analysis, fairly rare."

The examples of phyletic gradualism produced by paleontologists from a wide variety of fossil groups are often presented not only as examples of gradual morphological transformation over time, but also as examples of speciation, in other words the production of new species. This kind of statement conceals a semantic trap. A paleontological species is a historical and chronological concept based on morphological resemblance; a biological species is a spatial and ecological concept based on genetic cohesion. But even if the genetic cohesion of the chronological species can only be inferred, comparing paleontological examples *to one another* is still entirely valid—the postulated units can be called species, chronospecies, paleospecies, chronological subspecies, transients, or whatever you like. Phyletic production of a new entity must be viewed as the production of something morphologically different, which therefore evolved; never mind whether what was produced can or cannot be categorized as a "species."

This gradualist model of phyletic speciation conflicts, however, with the "geographic speciation" model, favored by biologists who follow the lead of the American zoologist Ernst Mayr, one of the creators of the synthetic theory of evolution which forms the neo-Darwinian framework of modern biology. I will not address the tremendous question of "actualist" models of speciation (those based on present-day species). Suffice it to say that the geographic speciation model implies that new species appear from local populations located at the edges of the geographical distribution of the parent species; these are called "peripheral" populations. If geographical isolation leads to the genetic isolation of a peripheral population, it will experience an unprecedented degree of genetic mixing. If the geographical barrier then breaks down and the representatives of the peripheral population once again come into contact with the members of the main population, they will no longer be able to interbreed. A new species has arisen.

As emphasized by the British zoologist Richard Dawkins, one of the most intransigent of the neo-Darwinians, "the theory of speciation resulting from initial geographical separation has long been a cornerstone of mainstream, orthodox neo-Darwinism, and it is still accepted on all sides as the main process by which new species come into existence (some people think there are others as well)."[*] This

---

[*] Richard Dawkins, *The Blind Watchmaker* (W. W. Norton, New York, 1986), p. 239.

"cornerstone" makes no allowance for the possibility of progressive evolution *in situ* from one species to another, as shown by the phyletic speciation diagrams.

Eldredge and Gould have each tried to resolve this contradiction by applying the geographic speciation model to the fossil record, the former with reference to the evolution of a species of Devonian trilobite, *Phacops rana*, the latter by examining a species of Pleistocene snail, *Poecilozonites bermudensis*. Their conclusions were unequivocal: phyletic gradualism was, at best, grossly overrated. Speciation occurred instead by rapid transformation of peripheral populations: periods of rapid evolution punctuated much longer periods of equilibrium, or "stasis."

One of the essential criticisms leveled at the phyletic gradualism model by adherents of punctuated equilibrium concerns the geographic dimension of the question. Many examples of phyletic gradualism postulate a succession of species or populations without accounting for the geographical extent of the species, or for populations recognized at the different epochs in question. The species studied in a particular sedimentary basin are often found to be present in others; if fluctuations in the geographical distributions of the species are not taken into account, the phyletic lineages will give an incomplete, or even erroneous, explanation of the evolutionary process.

According to Eldredge and Gould, long periods of immobility are in fact the principal characteristic of a species over time. Stasis is a fact! they shout. There could be no better way to overturn the orthodox neo-Darwinian dogma of progressive and gradual evolution, although there is a certain problem of chronological scale to which I will return. On the other hand, the result is that the message of the fossils has unquestionably been upset: the paleontological documents did not necessarily support the model of phyletic gradualism. The two examples that I will now quickly summarize cannot be expected to produce any spectacular evolutionary changes; in fact the characteristics involved might seem trivial. But so it goes with evolutionary theory: little causes, great effects; little phenomena, great syntheses.

The trilobite *Phacops rana*, like every member of the phacopid family, had quite extraordinary eyes, very different from those of arthropods in general and other trilobites in particular. Its eye consisted of dozens, even hundreds, of lenses arranged in vertical bands. Each lens had its own cornea, so the eye was more like an aggregation of many independent eyes. In the 1960s, by preparing serial sections through the calcite of fossil lenses and examining them with a scanning electron microscope, researchers reconstructed the physiology of vision in these animals, and found that these trilobites could see a full 360° around themselves. The size and position of the eyes on the head, and the number of lenses, varied throughout the evolutionary history of the phacopids. Changes in the number of vertical bands of lenses in populations of *Phacops rana* from the Middle Devonian of North America were the key to understanding the evolution of this species. At this period, the eastern half of North America was covered by a shallow epicontinental sea; the continent itself (where the Appalachians were still rising) appeared above water only along what is now the east coast, which at that time was joined to Morocco, Scotland, Greenland, and Scandinavia. The Atlantic Ocean and the Mediterranean did not exist.

The fossils that allow us to follow the evolution of *Phacops rana* extended over eight million years. These trilobites were collected on the one hand from sediments deposited by the epicontinental sea—the principal distribution region (in present-day Michigan, Ohio, and Ontario)—and on the other hand from what is called the marginal region, a deep furrow along the continent (in New York state, farther to the east). The trilobite succession in the epicontinental sea deposits shows a decrease in the number of eye lens bands from eighteen to fifteen: a population with fifteen bands followed a population with twenty-seven bands, which in turn had succeeded a population with eighteen bands. Comparison with other *Phacops* has shown that the presence of eighteen bands represents the primitive state. No change in the number of bands was evident within each of the populations that succeeded one another in the epicontinental sea deposits. These changes appeared only in the trilobite populations discovered in the marginal zone farther east, along the Appalachians. What is more, the twenty-seven-band populations had emerged—quickly—well before they appeared in the great sea to the west. For more than two million years, the twenty-seven-band *Phacops* had been contemporary with the eighteen-band *Phacops*, but they lived elsewhere.

The phenomenon was repeated a bit later with the fifteen-band marginal populations. Two episodes of marine regression, followed by a return of the sea, influenced the epicontinental sea deposits. The *Phacops rana* populations characterized by a reduction in the number of lenses, which originally became differentiated in the marginal regions, subsequently moved into the epicontinental region, taking advantage of the return of the sea to replace the populations that had lived there previously. There was no gradual transformation *in situ* in the epicontinental region. The species *Phacops rana* was a stable species, in "stasis," and evolution occurred rapidly in the marginal populations, in accordance with the geographic speciation model.

The snail *Poecilozonites bermudensis* evolved in the Bermuda islands—in isolation—over the last 300,000 years in a similar manner. Climatic oscillations were severe during the Quaternary epoch, and the morphological changes in the Bermuda snail are interpreted in terms of climatic adaptations. The geographical distribution of these snails over time shows that the new populations (four of them) rapidly took on individual characteristics in regions peripheral to the principal region. This time, by examining the development of the shell, we can attribute these changes to instances of "pedomorphism," in which juvenile traits persist in the adult. In this case the descendant's shell no longer grows as the ancestor's shell did: it simply amplifies the initial stages of development. Conclusion: evolution from the ancestor to the descendant did not occur gradually in the principal region.

In these two paleontological studies, an almost literal reading of the fossil documents showed that a species is normally in "stasis," and that this equilibrium is rapidly punctuated by transformations that involve marginal, or peripheral, populations. Hence the model of "punctuated equilibrium." Other applications have followed, using animals as different as trilobites, molluscs, and antelope. For example, the French paleontologist Jean-Louis Henry, a famous hunter of trilobites in Brittany, has concluded that the evolution of Ordovician trilobites in the Armorican massif (involving species older than those studied by Eldredge) conforms to the model of punctuated equilibrium.

In addition, Eldredge and Gould found their model confirmed in a way—perhaps unexpectedly—by research in theoretical genetics. In 1932, the American geneticist Sewall Wright (1889–1988), one of the founders of population genetics, had advanced the notion of an "adaptive landscape," one of whose repercussions was to influence Simpson's concept of quantum evolution that we discussed earlier. The adaptive landscape idea applied to examinations of multiple combinations of alleles (an allele is a single gene in several forms) in individuals. Some combinations would of course be more favorable than others. On a map, these favorable combinations would look like peaks; the less favorable ones would look like valleys. The theory was rapidly adapted to populations and species, with the peak then corresponding to the species' place in the adaptive landscape. In the 1980s, mathematical models were proposed, and were judged (by Wright himself, among others) to be consistent with the concepts of stasis and rapid transformation implied by punctuated equilibrium. The transition from one peak to another, in other words across a "non-adaptive" region (the valley), might be due to rapid genetic drift in which natural selection played no part; then, as soon as the upward slope of the other peak had been reached, selection would rapidly "pull" the population towards the summit. There was now a new alliance between two heterodox models, one emerging from theoretical genetics and the other from paleontology.

But not all paleontological documents can be examined in the light of the competing speciation models. Although the gaps resulting from the random nature of fossilization may have been overrated, they do exist. The research that I have conducted on the evolution of the order Proboscidea—animals with trunks, otherwise known as elephants—have not led me to decide unequivocally one way or the other. Even for the Miocene (a period extending from 24 to 5 million years ago, for which fossil mammals are not rare), the mesh of the fossilization net is much too coarse and the remains of Proboscidea are not plentiful enough. Nevertheless, working on the scale of the entire Old World, and at a taxonomic level higher than that of populations and sequences of species, I perceived that the evolutionary events in question were faster than had generally been thought.

An examination of the two living species (the Asian and African elephants) gives no inkling of the diversity of proboscideans in the Miocene, or even of the variety of elephantoids (forms similar to elephants, also called mastodonts). The diversification of these animals, as we understand its broad outlines, already provides some answers about evolutionary tempo. The four great natural groups, three of them known only from fossils, probably became established over a period of two million years at the base of the Miocene. The evolution of the major structures—spaced out, we believe, over almost ten million years—certainly took less than half as long. Different characteristics have different evolutionary tempi, and for some of them stasis was a reality.

The mammutids constitute one of these natural groups of mastodonts; despite their name, they should not be confused with the mammoths. I was fortunate enough to describe the first known representative of this group. They lived 22 million years ago in East Africa, in the oldest known African Miocene deposit, discovered by the British geologist Martin Pickford. The last species of mammutids died out in North America, a bit more than 10,000 years ago. During this interval, the mammutids penetrated into Eurasia, taking advantage of the collision between that continent and Africa, and then into the Americas across the Bering Strait, helped by oscillations in sea level. They lived in hot tropical environments and in temperate or cold climates, in dense forests, wooded savannas, grasslands, and spruce forests. Their molars exhibited practically no evolution. Someone unfamiliar with these animals would find it impossible to distinguish between a molar from species that lived 15 million years ago in France, and one from a species that lived 15,000 years ago in North America. Environmental selection pressures had no effect: stasis is a reality.

At the same time, in mastodon species more closely related to elephants that lived in the same environments, the molars evolved in spectacular fashion: this time even the rankest amateur could not possibly confuse the molars from a species that lived 15 million years ago in France with those of a species that lived 15,000 years ago in North America, or in Europe, Asia, or Africa. On the other hand, the jaws and tusks did undergo perceptible changes in the mammutids (in much the same way they did in elephants). We must conclude from these examples that evolutionary tempi are not the same for the species of a given group, or for the characteristics of a given species.

Eldredge and Gould were in fact interested in two subtly different subjects, and the fact that they are often amalgamated has become a source of confusion. The first topic involves the intrinsic information provided by the fossil record: the gaps are not as frequent as claimed, and an examination of the fossils supports both the geographic speciation model and the image of quantum (rapid) evolution conjured up by Simpson. The second involves evolutionary modes: although periods of speciation are rapid in terms of geological time, the hiatus that we see between the anatomies of various related organisms may be attributable to the evolutionary process itself. Major morphological transformations were apparently taking root quickly. Macroevolution is thus decoupled from microevolution. In this case the evolutionary process responsible for these hiatuses involves mutations which affect the "genes involved in controlling the form as derived from all of the cellular interactions."[*] These genes can be among those which control the rhythm of development. These modifications change the tempo of that development (heterochronism), and thereby change the final morphology. I should emphasize immediately that identification of large-scale evolutionary processes is not in any way the source of the model of punctuated equilibrium, even though the rebirth of macroevolutionary theories is linked to that model.

Eldredge and Gould's propositions had an enormous impact on neo-Darwinian orthodoxy. Evolutionists were definitely not pleased when told that the paleontological archives did not support the idea of gradual evolution, and that rapid, far-reaching morphological transformations had therefore occurred. The application, in paleontology, of the orthodox neo-Darwinian model of geographic speciation caused an uproar—a somewhat paradoxical situation. As for the revival of macroevolutionary theories, it scandalized more than one biologist: evolution had to be explained, they thought, solely by the processes of microevolution as revealed by

---

[*] Alain Prochaintz, *How the Brain Evolved,* New York, McGraw-Hill (1992), p. 46.

genetics (in other words, the gradual, progressive natural selection of variations within the species).

Paleontologists and geneticists do not have the same concept of time. According to the punctuated equilibrium model, speciation is a sudden event, taking between 5,000 and 50,000 years. On the geologic time scale, this is a rapid change that is difficult to discern in the paleontological records; but on the reproductive time scale it is a slow process. That is why, according to the orthodox neo-Darwinian biologists, the punctuated equilibrium model can quite easily fit into the gradualist framework of neo-Darwinism: there is no reason to postulate specific macroevolutionary processes in order to explain evolutionary changes, even punctuated ones. The criticism leveled at Eldredge and Gould by many paleontologists, however, is very different: gradual transformations extending over millions of years (rather than thousands) are in fact real, and not, as they claim, mere artifacts.

The discussions and controversies that swirl around these two ideas of evolutionary tempo have been very bitter, and they are not over yet. In the early 1980s, France's CNRS (National Center for Scientific Research) even organized an international colloquium to prove that the "punctuationists" were wrong. My contribution to this colloquium, in collaboration with my colleagues Daniel Goujet, Philippe Janvier, and Jean-Claude Rage, was worthy of the aggressiveness we had learned from the cladists: before quibbling about evolutionary tempos, we suggested, it would first be a good idea to establish reliable hypotheses about genealogical relationships. In some cases evolutionary scenarios, gradualist or otherwise, have in fact been refuted on cladistic grounds, or have turned out to be only one of numerous other equally plausible solutions.

Just as research on the Ordovician trilobites of the Armorican massif mentioned earlier was providing support for the punctuated equilibrium model, disagreement continued about other Ordovician trilobites, this time from Wales. The episode is worth looking at in detail, because it sheds a great deal of light on the stakes (scientific and otherwise) of this debate.

The eight lineages of Welsh trilobites studied by the British paleontologist Peter Sheldon evolved gradually. The characteristic examined this time was the number of ribs on the posterior part of the body. This number, analyzed over a period of three million years, increased globally within each lineage (with "reversions" within five lineages, in other words periods during which the number of ribs decreased before again increasing). This result was touted in neo-Darwinian circles as a refutation of the punctuated equilibrium model. "Darwinism remains unpunctuated," remarked the British evolutionist

John Maynard Smith. "But punctuated equilibrium predominates," retorted Eldredge and Gould.

In their response, Eldredge and Gould emphasized an important point concerning the rates of evolution implied by phyletic lineages, whether Welsh trilobites or other examples of phyletic gradualism (terrestrial mammals, in particular). If they were to account for all the morphological diversity of the groups in question, these transformation rates would require evolutionary time spans infinitely longer than the periods during which the groups were known. One must therefore postulate periods when major morphological features became rapidly established! Leaving aside a debate about selection among species, which I will not go into here, agreement was reached on the tempo of evolution. In his final commentary, Maynard Smith acknowledged that stasis was a real phenomenon, and that different speciation rates might be responsible for taxonomic diversity; but he concluded that all that was perfectly consistent with neo-Darwinian ideas. Along the way, the promoters of punctuated equilibrium had in fact once written "[…] we are all Darwinians […]": that said it all! "Welcome back!" came the response from their colleagues.

This exchange clearly reveals the extrascientific implications of the controversy. Over the years, Eldredge and Gould had been accused of mounting a frontal attack on neo-Darwinism (which is indisputable); by so doing, they laid themselves open to accusations of being antievolutionists (which is debatable). This is a paradoxical situation for two paleontologists fighting on the front lines of an interminable and courageous battle against the American creationist movement. But the neo-Darwinian citadel is so constructed that nothing having to do with evolution can claim to lie beyond it: by announcing the advent of a new paradigm, by reviving the old heretical notion of macroevolution, Gould had gone too far.

BACK TO THE EMBRYO

The revival of macroevolution owes much to another resurrection: that of research on ontogeny, or development of the individual. Gould has been an ardent promoter of such research, long neglected by most architects of the neo-Darwinian synthesis. It might be regarded as a means of reconciling the evolutionary processes seen by paleontologists with the mechanisms considered by geneticists.

The development of an individual passes through several phases in which characteristics develop from the embryo to the adult stage. These transformations occur according to a precise chronology, and changes in this chronology can result in perceptible morphological alterations. The differentiation of new species can therefore be induced by these changes in development. In the case of *Poecilozonites*, the Bermuda snail, an early halt in development seems to be responsible for amplification, in the adult stage, of juvenile traits. In other cases, and perhaps more frequently, it is accelerated development or extended implementation time that are responsible for morphological transformations. These various phenomena involving changes in the rhythm of ontogenic development are called "heterochronic."

Although the concept of heterochronic effects was developed in the last century by Haeckel and explored forty years ago by the British biologist Sir Gavin de Beer (1899–1972), it was seldom called upon. Only recently has it begun to crop up in the paleontological literature, but today, developmental analyses are being made of every zoological group.

Among the amphibians, living salamanders offer numerous cases of arrested or slowed development (pedomorphism). An obvious feature in the metamorphosis of amphibians (a well-researched phenomenon) is loss of the gills. But in certain cases pedomorphosis causes gills to persist in the adult. Such instances are seen in a number of fossil amphibians—the stegocephalids—represented by highly ossified forms that can sometimes reach ten feet in length. There are several large adult forms in which the skeleton of the gills is perfectly ossified.

Abundant during the Paleozoic era, the stegocephalids became rarer during the Mesozoic; a number of them are pedomorphs. This is especially true for the more recent species (the plagiosaurs of the Cretaceous). Analogous mechanisms have also been described in several groups of invertebrates, such as Tertiary sea urchins and Jurassic ammonites.

Mechanisms acting in the opposite direction—acceleration of the rate of development or extension of development time—lead to new morphologies which look like extreme derivatives of the preceding structures, and affect every group. In addition, certain spectacular structures, like the extraordinarily large antlers of the giant Irish elk that lived in the Quaternary, can easily be explained by an exponential growth relationship between the stag's body size and the size of its antlers. If the modern red deer, now common in Europe, grew to the height of the giant elk (1.80 m, or about 6 feet at the withers), its antlers would also be as large as those of the great fossil stag!

It is possible to establish, by means of development genetics, a link between the major morphological transformations observed by paleontologists, and the microevolutionary processes detected by geneticists. If a mutation affects a regulator gene controlling the tempo at which an organ develops, the organ will be altered and the resulting morphology will necessarily be transformed. The change involved may be considerable. If we assume that periods of speciation are short, major morphological changes would thus become fixed without leaving any trace that we could perceive in the fossil documents, since fossil-bearing sediments rarely offer the paleontologist a succession of deposits ranging over a period of 5,000 to 50,000 years. The idea that emerges is therefore of substantial "quantum" transformations, almost instantaneous on a geological scale if not in terms of reproduction. The entire problem then comes down to explaining how these transformations are perpetuated within necessarily small populations. There is, needless to say, no lack of controversy on the subject.

Turning to birds, the Jurassic *Archaeopteryx* has a complete fibula similar to that of its close dinosaur relatives. It has been known since the 1950s that a chick embryo can be experimentally induced to form a complete fibula instead of the thin needle, unattached at one end, that it usually has. The program by which the morphology of a bird fibula is constructed therefore retains a certain plasticity, despite the changes that it underwent more than a hundred million years ago. But developmental alterations do not all necessarily result from genetic causes. Influenced by environmental conditions, often by way of hormones which inhibit or activate the process, they are then called "epigenetic." This entire field of biology is presently developing rapidly; it is not as unconnected with paleontological research as one might first think.

The upshot of these debates about the tempo of evolution is that very probably, both gradualism and punctuation have affected evolution. The question of which of the two processes predominated still remains open for investigation, but contrary to the claims of traditional Darwinian literature, we find that stasis does exist and provides a sharply contrasting backdrop to periods of transformation. We might sum up, from a punctuationist point of view, with a paradox: evolution is possible because, for most of their existence, species do not evolve.

INTERMEDIATES

One reads very frequently that paleontology offers few intermediates, forms that illustrate the transition between anatomically distinct organizations. One of the principal arguments against evolution is indeed the supposed rarity of such transitional forms. But in fact, the discussion here is completely off the point. The intermediate fossil species, an almost mythical entity if one assumes that the notion of "missing links" is absolutely true, is generally poorly understood.

What is the conventional view of this intermediate? As a half-and-half organism, of course.

Inevitably—and intuitively, after all—we look for intermediates between the major groups in order to find symbols of evolution. So we would look for the transitional form between fish and amphibians, or perhaps between reptiles and birds, or reptiles and mammals, or even between apes and humans, trying to find a being that was half fish and half amphibian, half reptile and half bird, etc. This is a senseless undertaking. Without the slightest ambiguity, the fossils repudiate this type of poorly framed question.

An empirical observation of fossils reveals that it is always one characteristic or one type of characteristic that evolves at a given rhythm, rather than the entire morphology. Whether the phyletic gradualism of the ribs of Ordovician trilobites or the "punctuationism" of eye lenses in Devonian trilobites, in each instance only a single very precise characteristic is involved. As we have seen, analyses of fossils show that in a natural group, characteristics evolve independently. This almost universal finding can easily be explained by selection processes: the adaptive response of a population to environmental changes will affect the dental apparatus, the locomotor system, or perhaps vision, depending on the case. As subsequent speciation takes place, these transformations are transmitted, become modified in turn, or may even remain unchanged. The result, within any given species, is an association of characteristics exhibiting a variety of evolutionary levels; this has

been called "mosaic evolution," an expression proposed by de Beer almost forty years ago with
reference to *Archaeopteryx*. What we have just
learned about the role of peripheral populations in
the emergence of new species implies that small marginal populations—ancestors, in the strict sense—
have a slim chance of leaving fossil remains. But fossils displaying intermediate, sketchy, emergent
characteristics are much less rare. The discovery of
species that are generally primitive in terms of many
characteristics but are already evolved in terms of
others, or even a single one, forces us to acknowledge the emergence of new groups without falling
back on half-and-half beings.

 Archaeopteryx, the first bird, which lived 140
million years ago in Europe, represents the prototype
of the intermediate fossil, since it connects two very
distant large groups, the reptiles and birds. But while
its "reptilian" characteristics are extremely numerous (it has teeth, claws on its wings, etc.), its birdlike
characteristics are very few. But if only because it
has feathers (whose fossilized imprint is visible on
several of the specimens discovered so far), the animal can unequivocally be considered a bird. It is an
extremely primitive bird in terms of most of its characteristics; and it is by no means half reptile and half
bird. In reality, its reptilian traits are still those of the
dinosaurs; but in the course of the Jurassic the selection of a few skeletal features, and the conversion of

scales into feathers, was enough to turn this dinosaur into a bird.

The search for half-and-half species is thus not only doomed to failure, but also completely alien to what we know about evolution. A few examples from the group with which I am most familiar, the proboscideans, will complete the reasoning. However strange it might seem, modern elephants are close relatives of aquatic mammals that are members of the order Sirenia, more commonly called "sea cows" (these sea cows have nothing to do with European "sea lambs," which are seals, and were once common along the Atlantic coast). This order includes the freshwater manatees of Africa and the Americas, and the dugong of the Indian Ocean. These animals have an elongated body, a massive, apparently neckless head, and front limbs transformed into paddles; they have lost their hind limbs, and have only a tail fin.

One would search in vain through the geological strata for a being half elephant, half sirenian. But an examination of the fossils, feature by feature, has shown that the first known species belonging to the order Sirenia and the order Proboscidea date back more than 40 million years. The divergence between them is undoubtedly far more ancient. These animals lived on the shores of the ancient Tethys Sea, an ocean which at that time joined the Atlantic to the Indian Ocean between Africa and Eurasia, since the

Arabia-Africa plate had not yet collided with Eurasia. Fossils of these animals have been discovered in Egypt, Libya, and Algeria, and, for the sirenians, as far away as Jamaica. The proboscidean species at this epoch bore very little resemblance to elephants, but the first sirenians look much more similar to their living descendants. Even more interesting is the observation that in terms of a number of skeletal characteristics, in particular the structure of the skull, the first proboscideans are more similar to the first sirenians than to their elephantine descendants.

The evolutionary conclusions are simple: Leaving aside the adaptations for swimming, we can state that elephants have diverged more, in certain respects, from the common ancestor that they share with the sirenians, than the sirenians themselves have. The *Moeritherium* genus of African proboscideans, with its long, low cranium, simple teeth, elongated body, and short limbs, did not look like an elephant. In general terms its cranium was very similar to that of a sirenian, but certain very subtle cranial characteristics, known only in elephants, are enough for taxonomic identification. The most primitive known proboscidean therefore constitutes a sort of intermediate between elephants and sirenians, but it is not half one and half the other. In addition, the first proboscidean species known from Africa and the Arabian peninsula between thirty and forty million years ago were already diversified and very different from one another, indicating an earlier evolution of which we still know nothing.

It is difficult to find a common denominator among these species, which means that a few features of the skull and limbs take on inestimable value. A few years ago I had the opportunity to propose a key feature for the proboscideans: it is located on the astragalus, one of the ankle bones. You might well be surprised that the first proboscideans can be recognized by their ankles and not, for example, by their trunk (or at least by the associated cranial structures). But this latter criterion, no matter how well entrenched in the anatomical vocabulary of paleontology, is not justified by the evidence—the first "trunk-bearers" in fact had no trunk! Moreover, because the first sirenians and the first proboscideans shared a number of characteristics that had not yet become specialized, they were also not much different from other mammals living at that period. We now begin to understand why it is so difficult to identify the first representatives of the large groups; the only reason the groups look so different to us is that their living species have been accumulating morphological changes over tens of millions of years.

Transitional forms can even be found in the fossil state in the absence of clearly resolved relationships among groups; one superb example is the origin of whales. The cetaceans have diverged morphologically further than any other mammal from the ancestral species common to all mammals (much further than *Homo sapiens*, for example). Ever since the Eocene (between 55 and 34 million years ago), the first known cetaceans occur as very large marine forms that give no apparent hint of their terrestrial origin. The affinities of this group are also still enigmatic, although a number of paleontologists propose —on the basis of dentition—that an entirely extinct group of terrestrial carnivores called mesonychids might be the ancestors of the whales. These fossils are classified alongside the artiodactyls. At present the artiodactyls, highly diversified herbivorous mammals, look like pigs, hippopotamuses, camels and giraffes, deer, and antelopes. In these animals the axis of the hand and foot passes between the third and fourth digits, an arrangement unique among mammals. In the summer of 1990, the American paleontologist Philip Gingerich and his co-workers described the skeleton of the foot of one of the first cetaceans. It was a revelation, instantly documenting the terrestrial past of these animals; it can also be considered an absolutely splendid intermediate. The animal was over 50 feet long, but the rear limb measured only some 20 inches. The axis of the foot passed between the third and fourth digits. This time the fossil confirmed the paleontologists' hypotheses.

One example of an absolute evolutionary break that was occasionally cited about forty years ago was the transition from reptiles to mammals. If one looks only at osteological data, mammals are particularly characterized by the existence of tiny bones in the middle ear and, concomitantly, by a completely original type of articulation between the lower jaw and the cranium. We now know of a whole series of transitional fossil amniotes—the mammalian reptiles—which exhibit mammalian traits, first sketched out and later affirmed, in this area. In other words, the transformation of the lower jaw and the development of the middle ear bones are no longer a mystery, but one of the nicest examples of biological evolution offered by the fossils. These intermediates lived from the Permian (295 million years ago) to the Jurassic (205 million years ago), the date at which the first true mammals can be identified. The fossils have definitively erased the presumed break.

So intermediate species, "missing links," do indeed exist, contrary to what is occasionally said and written. The only problem is that most of the time, we are not looking for what we should be looking for, because the intermediates are not intuitive ones. One must be sensitive to anatomical arguments in order to detect them, and it is not always easy to suppress the baneful image of the half-and-half. But there are some shining examples. The famous Lucy, the *Australopithecus* specimen from the Afar region of Ethiopia that lived more than three million years ago in Africa, was barely more than three feet tall. Her jaws and teeth were powerful; her brain was small (400 cubic centimeters, tiny compared to the 1400 cc of modern humans), her arms relatively long, and her legs short. But she was already bipedal: her feet, knees, and pelvis were human. Could there be any better intermediate between chimpanzees and humans?

III

CHANCE

AND HISTORY

Textbooks dealing with the theory of evolution often address the idea of contingency, a notion that has nevertheless always aroused a certain suspicion among evolutionists. It is only in a recent book by Stephen Jay Gould, *Wonderful Life*, that one finds a veritable monument erected in its honor. Having presented, in epic style, the Cambrian Burgess Shale fauna discussed earlier, Gould takes up arms against the epistemological habits that inspired a certain condescension towards the historical sciences among many evolutionists; he even proposes as his slogan, "Just history."

In a previous book[*], I had occasion to address some specific aspects of phylogenetic research, in other words the construction of genealogical trees. I will discuss it only briefly here. These trees show the stages in the diversification of living beings over time; they are historical representations. Now only a single evolutionary history has existed; and even a partial understanding of this history demonstrates the

---

[*]*L'Arbre à remonter le temps* [Climbing the tree of time], Paris, Bourgois, 1991.

role of chance, of contingency, in the processes of diversification and extinction. A certain scenario concerning the origin of human beings is associated with certain geological events; change those events (climatic, ecological, or geographical), and another scenario emerges. This view of events injects considerable relativity into the centuries-old search for the "laws of evolution" (which has practically always met with failure), and also greatly diminishes the predictive value of the theory of evolution. It is also the reason why for many years, contingency has not received from evolutionists the consideration it deserved, because it presents a challenge to experimentation. What is known about the history of life is, however, not completely without interest for its own sake, nor without implications concerning the meaning of existence. Using a few paleontological examples, I will confine myself here to the history of life and to the realm of tangible things about which Gould has written.

No matter how incomplete they may be, phylogenetic trees incontrovertibly demonstrate that the two major evolutionary factors—taxonomic diversification and extinction—have indeed taken place, and that they are linked to geological phenomena (or even to extraterrestrial ones, as we shall see later). The history of the Earth and the history of life are inseparable, and to a certain extent the former has influenced the latter. We can regard diversity and extinction as the engines responsible for the unfolding, over time, of the tree of living beings; and fossils illuminate, sometimes in spectacular fashion, evolutionary histories and the role played by the hazards of geography.

TAXONOMIC DIVERSIFICATION AND THE ORIGIN OF HUMAN BEINGS

In early 1991, the American paleontologist Christopher Beard and his co-workers announced they had discovered several skulls of a small North American primate. A routine paleontological item, one might think, except that the fossil in question was specifically a primate, the order of mammals to which human beings belong.

A few months earlier, the French paleontologist Bernard Sigé and his co-workers at Montpellier had described a dozen tiny teeth discovered in Morocco, also belonging to a primate. These two primates, one American and the other Moroccan, were more than fifty million years old. What linked them was not their age, however, but their place in the evolution of apes, and therefore of humans. These two discoveries are singularly important for anyone wishing to understand the history of the primates.

The skulls of the North American primate, discovered in sediments of early Tertiary date (Lower

Eocene, to be precise) in Wyoming, belonged to a species called *Shoshonius cooperi*, previously known only by its teeth. The skulls were just over an inch long, but so perfectly preserved that many detailed observations could be made, especially in the auditory region, a very valuable area in terms of speciation because of its relative stability. This analysis led to a fairly precise identification of the genealogical position of this species: *Shoshonius* was an omomyid, a group known only from fossils and closely related to modern tarsiers.

A few taxonomic explanations are in order here. Tarsiers are small nocturnal primates, with very large eyes and bodies adapted for jumping, that live in the forests of Southeast Asia; the ends of their hind limbs—an area called the tarsus, which gives these primates their name—are extremely elongated. Now very rare, these animals occupy a pivotal position in the evolution of the primates, a position that has aroused lively controversy. It is believed today, on the basis of both anatomical and genetic data, that they are closely related to the apes; they are said to be "sibling species." Apes and tarsiers together constitute the group of "haplorhines." Humans themselves are classified among the apes, in other words as "simiidae" or "anthropoids" depending on which nomenclature is used, since the two terms are synonymous.

The omomyids are generally regarded as the stock from which modern tarsiers emerged. The cranial anatomy of *Shoshonius* confirmed this hypothesis, and even better, *Shoshonius* turns out to be the omomyid that is closest to the tarsiers. But the most ancient known tarsier, *Tarsius thailandica*, the identification of which is no longer subject to debate, was described by the French paleontologists Léonard Ginsburg and Pierre Mein from the Miocene of Thailand, in other words in strata 30 million years younger. This sort of hiatus emphasizes the problem of gaps in fossilization, but fortunately anatomical comparisons can be used to bridge them to some extent.

Now that these paleontological points have been made, we can sketch out a picture of world geography 50 million years ago; thanks to our understanding of plate tectonics, the data today are quite accurate. The North Atlantic had not yet opened completely: North America and Europe were still united, connected by what is now Greenland. The Eocene was apparently the last period in which these two continents were still only one, forming the ancient Northern Hemisphere continent called Laurasia. To the south, an ocean called the Tethys Sea joined the Atlantic and the Indian Ocean, separating Africa from Laurasia. It appears that although it was much narrower than today's Atlantic, the Tethys did indeed act as a barrier to terrestrial vertebrates. Temporary emergences, especially those caused by the Apulian plate located on the site of modern Italy, allowed animals to cross this barrier, but contacts were still sufficiently rare and sporadic for different faunas to develop and evolve independently on the northern and southern shores of the Tethys. Later on, only 20 million years ago, the Arabo-African and Asiatic plates collided, permanently closing off the Tethys Sea to the east (it survived as the Mediterranean to the west) and leaving the way open for large-scale faunal exchanges.

Beginning in the 1970s, the French paleontologist Robert Hoffstetter proposed a biogeographical scenario in which the Tethys played a determining role in the differentiation of the haplorhines into tarsiers and apes. All the omomyid primates and tarsiers came from the old Laurasian continent—North America, Europe, and Asia—while all the apes were African. Geographical separation would have allowed the two groups to evolve along their own evolutionary lines, from ancestors already present for some ten million years on either side of the Tethys Sea.

A number of studies set out to test this hypothesis. Excavations on either side of the ancient shores of the Tethys were—and still are—particularly active. That is why every discovery is minutely analyzed and discussed. Are there still no tarsiers from Africa? Did the Tethys really play any role in the evolution of primates and the emergence of the apes?

A tarsier discovered in Egypt in sediments of Oligocene age (about 33 million years ago) was described several years ago on the basis of a fragment of lower jaw, but its taxonomic identification was immediately questioned: the jaw in fact probably belonged to an ape. Very ancient apes (between 34 and 40 million years old) are in fact known from sediments on the southern shore of the Tethys, in Algeria, Egypt, and Oman in the Arabian peninsula. None of these apes has ever been discovered on the northern shore of the Tethys. These fossil apes, especially those found recently in Oman by the French paleontologist Herbert Thomas, can be regarded as the ancestors of all the apes, both those of Africa and those that left Africa for South America (as I will discuss later) and Eurasia.

If fossil omomyids and modern tarsiers can in fact be considered a sibling group of the apes, the common ancestor must necessarily have lived earlier than the first representative of each of the two groups; and if the first known fossil omomyid dates back 50 million years, the first ape must also necessarily be equally old. Having studied the affinities of the *Shoshonius* omomyid, Beard and his co-workers thus concluded that there was a gap of more than ten million years in the fossil record of the apes, since the oldest known apes were less than 40 million years old.

The little primate teeth from Morocco described by Bernard Sigé confirmed this conclusion beyond all expectations. They are much more ancient (Paleocene, between 65 and 55 million years ago), but they were attributed to an omomyid, a group that, as we have just seen, was exclusively from north of the Tethys. So, should the hypothesis about the differentiation of apes be reformulated? Not necessarily: as far as Sigé and his co-workers were concerned, no matter what its place in the classification, *Altiatlasius* (the name given to this primate) was in fact closer in genealogical terms to the apes. What counts in this instance is genealogical position rather than taxonomic niceties. This confirmed both the great age of the apes, and the place where the group originated (Africa). It even appeared that the apes were older than had been thought.

One should not, of course, overestimate the amount of information supplied by a few teeth. At the present state of our knowledge it might nonetheless legitimately be concluded, at the very least, that the long-ago Tethys Sea did indeed play a role in the differentiation of the primates called haplorhines. This group, of cosmopolitan origin, is subdivided into tarsiers (in the general sense) to the north of the Tethys, and apes to the south. If this barrier had not been "operative," the evolution of primates would have been very different.

But the random effects of environment did not stop influencing the history of the primates after the emergence of apes. To the contrary: all the evidence suggests that changes in climate and habitat at the end of the Miocene (5–10 million years ago) were not without some impact on the origin of humans. To jump ahead to the conclusion, let me simply say that if drought had not affected a large portion of the Earth's tropical regions starting in the Middle Miocene (approximately 15 million years ago), there certainly would be no human beings on this planet.

What happened was this: during the Miocene epoch, the dense forests of the Old and New Worlds began to thin out because of a general cooling trend. Many mammals "responded" as habitats became more open, and meadows and savannas expanded. The evolution of the horse in North America is the most famous example. Some species, beginning with ancestors who lived in the forests and ate leaves, penetrated into these new open environments. The most obvious marks of their adaptation are found in features associated with diet and locomotion. Grasses (the Gramineae that appeared at this time on the planet) are a highly abrasive food. The height of the molars in meadow horses, which grazed on grass, grew more rapidly to compensate for wear, probably in accordance with a classic process of natural selection. This adaptive type was also selected, simultaneously, in several other groups of mammals as genealogically distant as, for example, modern African gazelles and antelopes, and fossil glyptodonts, a group of giant armadillos in South America.

Apes took some time to respond to these changes in habitat. Arboreal and therefore conservative animals, apes ventured only very cautiously out of the forests. The eastern closure of the Tethys Sea, which was complete about 18 million years ago, allowed large-scale faunal exchanges between Africa and Eurasia, as we have seen. The proboscideans (especially the distant ancestors of the elephants) were the first to profit from these land bridges. The apes followed them two or three million years later, spreading out into Eurasia. Among these apes was the superfamily of the hominoids, which includes humans, chimpanzees, gorillas, orangutans, and modern gibbons. Just to digress for a moment, I cannot resist the opportunity to recall that the first fossil hominoid great ape ever discovered was found in the 19th century, at a quarry near Saint-Gaudens in southern France. Édouard Lartet (1801–1871), a jurist turned paleontologist, dubbed it *Dryopithecus*, "ape of the oak trees," since it did indeed live in a closed, wooded environment. Among the hominoids, the adaptive response to open environments was a thickening of the tooth enamel. This trait appears in the human lineage and in *Sivapithecus* and *Ramapithecus*, fossils contemporary with *Dryopithecus*.

About a dozen years ago, I had the opportunity to participate in a *Sivapithecus* hunt on the Potwar plateau in Pakistan. The primatologist David Pilbeam was leading the expedition, and I was there not for the apes but for the proboscideans that accompanied them, the so-called "mastodons." The big moment (and the big surprise) of this excavation season was the discovery of the face of a *Sivapithecus*: it looked almost like a little orangutan. What we had been looking for, however, was a hominid, since the theory at that time was that two savanna hominoids existed at the same time: *Sivapithecus* on the one hand, and the smaller *Ramapithecus*, which was believed to be the direct ancestor of the hominids. These animals, although very famous among primatologists, were known at that time only from jaw fragments and from isolated, thick-enameled teeth. The many discoveries made on the Potwar plateau led paleontologists to adopt a fundamental change in their interpretations. *Sivapithecus* and *Ramapithecus* were found to be more similar than we had thought— perhaps even the same species—and the hominid traits that they exhibited could no longer be attributed to a close genealogical relationship with the human lineage, but rather to simple convergence. Thick enamel, which had been thought to be characteristic of hominids, had therefore appeared independently in the human lineage and in a lineage of orangutans adapted to open environments. The publication of the face of *Sivapithecus* in 1982 stimulated new research on the origin of the hominids.

Today, paleontologists and molecular biologists agree as to the affinities of *Homo sapiens*. Humans are closely related to modern chimpanzees and gorillas, in other words to the African great apes. The first fossil humans, the australopithecines of about four million years ago, are also African. Although we must be careful never to underestimate the gaps in the fossil record, everything seems to indicate that hominids are of African origin. The French paleoanthropologist Yves Coppens has proposed an ecological theory—referred to genially as "East Side Story"—in which the Rift Valley of East Africa plays a primary and decisive role in the emergence of humanity.

No one has ever discovered a securely attributed fossil chimpanzee or gorilla. This can be explained by the fact that these arboreal animals have remained confined to the equatorial forests, those same forests that were home to their ancestor, the common ancestor of the African great apes and humans. But bones generally fossilize poorly in this type of environment, and sedimentary outcrops capable of yielding fossils are also extremely rare in the African forest. At the end of the Miocene, tectonic movements of the African Rift produced a veritable chasm in the landscape, with volcanoes arising on the edges of the subsiding trenches. To the east of the Rift, even at equatorial latitudes, environments were drier, and the savannas stretched as far as the eye could see; to the west, the humid forest remained. It was in the eastern savannas that our human ancestors took their first steps, like the *Sivapithecus* mentioned earlier. The difference in the success enjoyed by *Sivapithecus* and the australopithecines was probably due to bipedalism, which appeared only in the latter. But without the desiccation of the environment, which was particularly evident in East Africa, none of the African species of hominoids would have been tempted to venture outside the forests.

Primate fossils are rare as a general rule; primate enthusiasts, zoologists, paleontologists, and paleoanthropologists are rather less so. That is why news of the discovery of primate fossils arrives so regularly. But to give a precise idea of the place of primates within fossil faunas, it is enough to know that in the two deposits where they were discovered, the four skulls of the Wyoming *Shoshonius* mentioned earlier represented only a tiny portion of a fauna comprising no fewer than sixty-five other species of mammals. The discovery of a primate is therefore always remarkable and remarked upon. That is why the announcement in 1990 of the discovery of a hominoid cranium in sediments dating back to about 10 million years ago was so sensational, especially when its discoverer, the French paleontologist Louis de Bonis, presented it as the ancestor of the australopithecines. But most astonishing of all is that this animal (called *Ouranopithecus*), formerly known only from its teeth and jaws, lived in the Greek province of Macedonia—in an open environment, to be sure, but very far from the Rift Valley. Was the eastern limit of the ancestors of the australopithecines even farther east and north than had been thought? Or perhaps, like the *Sivapithecus* from which it was unambiguously different, had this animal acquired its savanna hominoid characteristics concurrently with the hominids? We still await a definitive answer but whatever it is, the appearance of a drier environment is responsible for the emergence of human beings.

We are not yet done with contingency. The very appearance of modern humans, *Homo sapiens sapiens*, is perhaps the result of geographical accident. A million years ago *Homo erectus*, our direct ancestor, was present throughout the Old World. The first known representatives of *Homo sapiens sapiens* were distributed south of the Mediterranean (from Morocco to the Middle East, including East Africa). In the Middle East, for example, the human skeletal material of Qafzeh in Israel, discovered by the French anthropologist Bernard Vandermeersch, have been dated to 90,000 years ago, first by an examination of small fossil mammals and then by absolute dating. Human beings have not changed physically for 90,000 years. Living at this time north of the Mediterranean were Neanderthals, *Homo sapiens neanderthalensis*, those humans who, as the French paleoanthropologist Anne-Marie Tillier has told us, could talk just like anyone else. The contact zone between these two populations was located in the Middle East. It appears probable that the sequence of cold climatic phases during the Quaternary in Western Europe, with the resulting changes in landscape, had isolated the *Homo sapiens* populations that had descended from *Homo erectus* to the point that Neanderthals and modern humans acquired individual characteristics on either side of the Mediterranean. Without these geographic and climatic circumstances, the physiognomy of Neanderthals and that of modern human beings might have been very different.

It therefore appears that the primates, as opportunistic as any living being, have retained traces of the history of the planet. The origins of humans are contingent on the role of the Tethys Sea, on desiccation of habitats east of the Rift Valley, or on glaciations in Europe. Nothing in the anatomy of Tertiary primates would allow us to predict the appearance of human beings. What is more, no evolutionary potential of the primates can be invoked to conclude that under other circumstances, human beings would ultimately have emerged anyway. The history of South American monkeys offers the key to this statement.

Let us go back to the period around 30 million years ago, at which we see the first apes starting to diversify in Africa and, oddly enough, arriving in South America. At this period, South America was isolated from the rest of the world. It was distinct from North America (since Central America did not exist yet), and it was separated from Africa by the Atlantic; an Atlantic certainly narrower than today but nonetheless a genuine ocean.

South American monkeys, of the suborder Platyrrhini, include spider-monkeys, howler monkeys, marmosets, kinkajous, and many other species, all of them arboreal. The routes taken by these monkeys in reaching Latin America remain enigmatic. Are they of North American origin? In that case they would have had to cross a wide stretch of water, and the prevailing east-west orientation of the currents is unfavorable. Moreover, no potential ancestor has ever been discovered in North America: all the primates discovered there belonged to primitive species not related to the platyrrhines. We do know, however, that at the present time, the Platyrrhini constitute a sibling group of the Old World monkeys, the catarrhines. It appears probable, therefore, that the Latin American monkeys are African in origin. Fossils discovered in Egypt (*Parapithecus*) are their plausible ancestors.

The South American fossil record is clear: the platyrrhines appear suddenly during the Oligocene (30–24 million years ago), accompanied by rodents (also related to African forms); the two are the only exotic mammals among fauna which were endemic (in other words had evolved *in situ*) and had been on the continent since the beginning of the Tertiary.

Independently of the history of the primates, we see here another example of the role of geography in the evolution of animal groups. With the exception of this incursion of monkeys and rodents 30 million years ago, South America had experienced, for some 50 million years, an evolutionary history that could be called *in vitro*. Its fauna was original: the sloths and armadillos, in particular, appear to be unique survivors of it.

The hypothesis advanced to explain the presence of monkeys and rodents from Africa in South America supposes that they crossed the Atlantic on natural rafts: a chunk of shoreline with a mass of trees is assumed to have broken away from the continent in some African estuary and reached South America. Such rafts do form sometimes, drifting out from the great estuaries such as that of the Amazon, but they disintegrate after a few hundred kilometers at the very most, and this sort of trans-Atlantic voyage strains credulity. Some writers assume that now-submerged islands, known from geological evidence, might have served as waystations on this odyssey. But there is no assurance that living conditions on volcanic mid-oceanic islands would have been conducive to the survival of primates.

Whatever the case, starting with the first known example of an Oligocene platyrrhine—genus *Branisella*, described by Robert Hoffstetter—monkeys diversified into all the ecological niches offered by a forest habitat. But desiccation of habitats affected South America as well. I have already mentioned that the glyptodonts, giant armadillos with rigid armor plating, adapted to these open environments by developing dental characteristics analogous to those seen in horses. The continual growth of glyptodont molars was, moreover, quite remarkable: their peg-shaped teeth grew to a length of about four inches. But unlike the situation in the Old World, not a single South American monkey adapted to the grassland habitats! The hominid "model," or even an approximation of it, did not appear: placed in comparable ecological conditions, these monkeys did not respond in the same way. Therefore, nothing predestined the primates to give rise to the hominids.

One might refute this statement by pointing out that the African catarrhines had in fact acquired characteristics unknown among South American primates. These characteristics range from ossification of the auditory region to the dental formula (catarrhines have 32 teeth, having lost two premolars per jaw). One might also note that within the catarrhines, some traits evolved only in the hominoids (the most obvious being undoubtedly the loss of the tail). Other, more subtle osteological features exist in hominoid fossils dating from about 20 million years ago; but these attributes all appeared in woodland species, species that obviously could not have known that one day their descendants would be called upon to evolve on the open savanna. Taking a teleological point of view, one might therefore regard these characteristics as "potentialities," part of a substrate implying inevitable future evolutionary events. For my part, though, I see in them only the inheritance gathered from ancestor species: the fruit of history, not preparation for the coming of the hominids.

The ascent of humans therefore comes down to certain singularly prosaic contingent factors: climatic changes, the position of the continents, the presence or absence of barriers—and no doubt a multitude of tiny random events whose details escape us—seem to have had much more impact on the evolution of living beings than the "evolutionary potential" ascribed to any particular group.

DINOSAURS AND MASS EXTINCTIONS

Diversification and extinction are an inseparable pair. But evolutionary factors have too often been simplified, reducing them to the repopulation of an ecological niche, left vacant by the extinction of a species belonging to group A, by a similarly adapted species belonging to group B. There is no arguing with the reality of this phenomenon, but it is not as automatic as we are sometimes led to believe. It is also a good idea to make a distinction between extinction as a generator of diversity, and extinction in the strict sense, which irrevocably reduces diversity. A species which becomes extinct because it has produced descendant species (= speciation) produces diversity (it has been transformed rather than being wiped out). A species that is erased without descendants, because of a variety of environmental changes, truly expresses the concept of extinction.

Mass extinctions constitute a special case. What is remarkable about them is that a large proportion of the species living at a given time, belonging to a variety of taxonomic groups, disappear simultaneously. The harmonious ecological balance is upset: competition between certain species can no longer be invoked to explain these extinctions, and they must be attributed to major extrinsic factors.

Mass extinctions do not seem to be at all exceptional on the scale of our planet's history, and large numbers of paleontologists, geologists, and geophysicists are presently in hot pursuit of the causes of these phenomena. Gould uses the word "decimation" when speaking of these periods of extinction: often the species that go extinct disappear not because of some adaptive weakness, but simply by chance or bad luck—they lost the lottery. This rather radical point of view does not represent the dominant opinion in the profession, but it is guided by an approach to the notion of progress as developed and applied in the evolutionary sciences, and forces us to make a short detour into the idea of adaptation, a concept that is often poorly understood.

Adaptation is only a transitory virtue. Species must adapt to an environment that is constantly changing: destroy a habitat, and you wipe out a species in thrall to that habitat. Explaining the event by saying that the species was not well adapted to the new environment simply means reiterating that the extinct species was associated with the previous environment. Deciding whether adaptations in either the modern or fossil world should be viewed as mere "making do"—a point of view to which I subscribe—or, on the contrary, as deliberate as fine watchmaking, depends a lot on subjectivity. Phylogenetic trees, on the other hand, exhibit a sort of race between living beings and environmental fluctuations; and it turns out that to deal with the most urgent problem, making do is often the best solution. The upshot is that it is difficult to associate the course of evolution with any concept of "progress."

The sad fate of the dinosaurs has always fascinated anyone who has looked into the history of life. These animals diversified for 150 million years, and throughout this impressively long period of time, some lineages went extinct and others emerged. The largest dinosaurs—and the best known, such as *Diplodocus*—vanished in the Jurassic, but they were replaced by other species. Why did the dinosaurs become extinct at the end of the Cretaceous, 65 million years ago? Why did the production of new species cease? Why did other groups disappear at the same time? In what way were the surviving groups "better adapted"?

For about the last ten years, the extinction of these "terrible lizards" has been without doubt the leading topic in media coverage of paleontological subjects. As a result, interest in the dinosaurs—which is as old as paleontology itself—has been revived and considerably expanded. Nevertheless, this success came not really from the work of paleontologists, but from that of physicists. In the early 1980s, the American physicist Luis Alvarez (1911–1988) and his co-workers, including his son Walter, discovered abnormally high levels of iridium in sediments marking the transition between the Cretaceous and Tertiary eras (known to specialists as the K–T boundary). It was then assumed that a source capable of enriching a sediment in iridium, a mineral that is rare on the Earth's surface, could only be of extraterrestrial origin. From this arose the hypothesis, by now quite familiar, that an asteroid (or a comet) struck the planet some 65 million years ago, scorching the surface of the continents and spewing a huge dust cloud into the atmosphere. The dust is believed to have prevented sunlight from reaching the Earth's surface; the temperature would then have dropped, photosynthesis would have shut down, and cold acid rain would have fallen. This "nuclear winter" before its time would have destroyed life on Earth. In this scenario, the principal phase of extinctions would have lasted no more than ten years, and a total of one thousand to five thousand years would have sufficed to sweep the dinosaurs, and other species of the Mesozoic era, from the land and sea. On the geologic scale, it would indeed have been an instantaneous event.

This catastrophist scenario and its chronology have since undergone some revisions, but before discussing then, and seeing if this hypothesis is really the only reasonable one, let us first ask the pivotal question: what do the fossils tell us about the matter? Does the image of mass extinction, viewed as a total extinction—particularly well illustrated in the case of the dinosaurs—really tally with the paleontological data? One might immediately answer "Yes," since no dinosaur has ever been discovered in deposits of Tertiary or Quaternary age: the dinosaurs, which did indeed disappear, have always been associated with the concept of extinction. But in fact the answer is very different. If we actually look at all the living organisms on land and sea at the end of the Cretaceous, we find that life did not simply stop from one day to the next. Or, if you prefer, the image suggesting that living beings, suffocated by what was falling on them, disappeared almost entirely except for a few species, especially the mammals—with whom the evolutionary process then started all over again—is quite simply wrong.

To summarize the paleontological data very briefly, the mass extinction at the end of the Cretaceous affected only 15% of the families of animals that lived at that time. That is quite a score from a biological point of view, but hardly likely to confirm the idea of a global catastrophe. Mammals, birds, lizards, snakes, crocodiles, turtles, and amphibians were unaffected by this "mass extinction." All these groups, present at that time, are still present today. In the sea, bryozoans, brachiopods, lamellibranchs, gastropods, echinoderms, and crustaceans were also relatively untouched by the extinction phenomena. But that does not mean that none of the species belonging to these groups disappeared. The distinction is important, since the organisms that responded to changes in their environment, whether due to terrestrial or extraterrestrial phenomena, were individuals and not categories of classification. But it is down at the level of families and genera containing a highly variable number of species that we find better statistics. For example, although no entire family of turtles or crocodiles disappeared at the K–T boundary, between 15 and 30% of the genera belonging to those families went extinct at that time. The bony fishes did not disappear, but 11 families (of 85 present at the time) disappeared in the Upper Cretaceous (the proportion is 13%; to specialists, "mass extinction" is a relative term). As far as life in the seas is concerned, statistical estimates have been made on the census of fossil marine families published by the American paleontologist John Sepkoski in 1982, and indicate that a third of the marine families vanished during the same period. This publication also proposed a model for the periodicity of mass extinctions, not just the late Cretaceous one, a topic to which I shall return later.

But even though the bias introduced by taxonomic generalizations must not be overlooked, the fact remains that entire groups went extinct, just like the dinosaurs. To get an idea of the magnitude of the phenomenon, we then need to ask two questions about the number of species involved and the pace of the extinctions. Were the groups that became extinct large ones? And was the mass extinction really sudden, or in fact gradual?

Answers to these questions come from a piece of enormously dedicated work on reptiles published in 1987 by the American paleontologist Robert Sullivan. He painstakingly surveyed these groups over a period ranging from the Upper Cretaceous to the Paleocene in the early Tertiary (87.5 to 54 million years ago). The investigation was made at the smallest taxonomic scale possible, down to the number of fossil specimens so far collected. He ended up analyzing forty-four families of reptiles represented at this period, along with seven fossil species that had never been classified. A total of 20% of these families became extinct at the K–T boundary. Of these forty-four families, twenty belonged to five large groups not represented among living animals: dinosaurs, pterosaurs (flying reptiles), ichthyosaurs and plesiosaurs (marine reptiles), and champsosaurs.

The fate of the champsosaurs was just as fascinating as that of the dinosaurs, although they have never had the same popular appeal. These semi-aquatic saurians were ten feet long; they looked a little like crocodiles, and their skull had a long snout and a very elongated temporal region. What does paleontology tell us about them? The champsosaurs passed through the K–T boundary without incident, and did not become extinct until the end of the Paleocene, or 9 million years after the supposed asteroid impact. The ichthyosaurs and plesiosaurs (with one single family represented for each group) had already become very rare in the Upper Cretaceous, and went extinct in the Campanian, at least 8 million years *before* the putative asteroid impact. Of the two pterosaur families, one did not survive the Campanian, while the other, which did indeed disappear at the K–T boundary, was by then represented by only three species.

As for the famous dinosaurs, they are represented in the Upper Cretaceous by fifteen families, to which we must add four species of uncertain affinities, each known from a single deposit (their very rarity thus excludes them from any statistical analysis of extinction modes). Of the fifteen families surveyed, only eight disappeared at the K–T boundary; two had become extinct 4 million years earlier; three disappeared 6 million years earlier; and the extinction of the last two goes back to the Campanian and Santonian, or 15–20 million years before the K–T boundary. The only dinosaurs that became instantaneously extinct were therefore those in the eight families, which is already not bad since they represent 53% of the families. But those eight families— the last of the dinosaurs—contained only twelve species for the last three million years of the Cretaceous (the Upper Maastrichtian). This meager showing is nothing like the number of dinosaur species that had lived previously; if we examine the older periods of the Upper Cretaceous, we can count between forty and eighty species during equivalent three-million-year periods. The terrestrial fauna therefore started to experience dinosaur depletion well before the K–T boundary.

Of course not every dinosaur has been discovered, and Sullivan also surveyed only New World species. The bias introduced by gaps in fossilization does really exist, and caution must be exercised when making statistical comparisons among sparse numbers. For example, of the twelve known last species of dinosaurs, only three had yielded more than ten specimens by 1987. The importance of this bias can nevertheless be seen in relative terms by noting that the fossil sample surviving of these last dinosaurs in the Upper Maastrichtian is equivalent to that in the Lower Maastrichtian or in earlier epochs of the Upper Cretaceous. Even if we acknowledge that the dinosaur species living at this period have not all been discovered by paleontologists, the same is also true for the earlier periods. In order for the fossils to be systematically deceiving us in this regard, the discoveries made for the terminal Maastrichtian and the previous periods must not be reflecting the true number of species in the same proportions; and there is no reason to think this is the case.

Sullivan's work should be compared with that of the American paleontologists William Clemens and David Archibald, who have made a detailed study of the stratigraphy of the North American formations (essentially those in Montana) that are very rich in dinosaurs and other continental species, and identified the extinction dates of the various groups. The picture that emerged from this precise analysis was of a progressive decline of the dinosaurs. Since these investigations involved sites on the North American continent, generalizations on a planetary scale would be foolhardy, but paleontological sites in Mongolia furnish a comparable example. Here, the dinosaur fauna from the latest Maastrichtian levels prove to be much less diverse than those at the beginning of the stage and in preceding stages. The fact remains, however, that geological formations of Upper Cretaceous age, and of sufficient thickness to support detailed analysis, are not very numerous.

Current research suggests a progressive local decline, with nothing to indicate that dinosaur extinctions were contemporaneous on a global scale. The disappearance of the dinosaurs in fact extends throughout the Maastrichtian, or over some ten million years. If we remember that three species of pterosaurs also disappeared at the K–T limit, the supposed extraterrestrial massacre would thus have affected only about fifteen species. Commenting on Sullivan's results, the British paleontologist Michael Benton, a specialist in dinosaurs and diversification/ extinction processes, asked ironically: "Is the loss of fifteen reptile species over three million years a catastrophic mass extinction?" Even if we concede that other species remain to be discovered, we are still far from seeing a global catastrophe suddenly wiping out the entire group of dinosaurs. In trying to understand the ways in which living things become extinct, the number of species and individuals counts for much more than taxonomic generalization.

Mass extinctions of plants are not observed at the Cretaceous–Tertiary boundary; instead we see local ecological readjustments. Fern pollen is very common in North America and Japan just after the K–T boundary; this is sometimes interpreted as a new and rapid colonization of the continents in a wet environment after a period of disturbance.

Marine invertebrate fossils offer us a picture just as different as the one redrawn on the basis of reptiles. It has been estimated that 45% of near-surface marine species and 20% of the species living in the ocean depths disappeared at the end of the Cretaceous. As a general rule, marine fossils are far more abundant than terrestrial ones; it is therefore easier to track their relative numbers through strati-graphic sections, and the bias introduced by the rarity of terrestrial vertebrates can be ignored in this case. It is true that many marine groups became extinct in the Upper Cretaceous, but most specialists agree that the pattern is gradual rather than catastrophic. These groups became less and less common during the Maastrichtian (over a period of some ten million years), and their last representatives did not survive to the K–T boundary, that is, the iridium deposit representing the signature of the putative asteroid impact.

The ammonites (cephalopods like the octopus) constitute the most famous group of fossil marine invertebrates known to collectors. They had a shell like that of the nautilus, their living relative that is a true refugee from the past. As a student, I was taught that ammonites did in fact disappear at the end of the Mesozoic, and that they shared the same fate as the dinosaurs. But ammonites became *progressively* rarer during the entire Upper Cretaceous, and the last representatives of the group disappeared *before* the

K–T boundary; their mass extinction was therefore not instantaneous. The same is true for the belemnites, another group of fossil cephalopods. The *Inoceramus* group—bivalves similar to oysters—did actually disappear at the K–T boundary, but they also had been getting scarcer over the last eight million years of the Cretaceous. Another group of molluscs called rudists, which were reef-building animals, was decimated at the end of the Cretaceous. Some of them were enormous, like the aptly named *Titanosarcolites giganteus*, which was over six feet long. The rudists lived in shallow tropical waters and were common in the Maastrichtian. Most of them had died out two million years before the K–T boundary, and the last rudists to fall victim to the mass extinction were rare and not highly diversified.

When we look at planktonic microfauna, however, we see truly catastrophic extinctions, which beyond any doubt were simultaneous over the entire surface of the Earth. The result was to reduce marine microplankton by two thirds. The planktonic foraminifera decreased in spectacular fashion: of the 36 species represented at the end of the Cretaceous, only one survived to the beginning of the Tertiary. Plankton is the foundation of the marine food chain, and any depletion of its ranks would inevitably have had profound effects on other marine groups. It was not without good reason that Alvarez and his co-workers associated the effects of the supposed asteroid impact with the extinction of plankton species. But the complexity and diversity of the extinction phenomena of the final Cretaceous, along with the well-established fact that no contemporary global extinction affected either the various marine or terrestrial fossil species, explain why most paleontologists have remained unconvinced by the catastrophist hypothesis that invokes an asteroid or comet impact. With the exception of the plankton, all the groups that became extinct at the end of the Maastrichtian had suffered a decline that can be described as slow inasmuch as a period of three to ten million years is long as far as biological phenomena are concerned. With reference to the dinosaurs, the American paleontologist Stephen Jay Gould has summarized the situation by describing the effect of the killer asteroid as a "coup de grâce" administered to a group that had already been severely thinned out. A search for the causes of that thinning would therefore seem to be just as important as any attempt to characterize the coup de grâce.

For other paleontologists, the effects of the great marine regressions at the end of the Cretaceous are sufficient explanation for the extinction of the dinosaurs and the other terrestrial and marine groups. Since the 1960s, the French paleontologist Léonard Ginsburg has been the chief advocate of this theory, which differs from those that invoke extraterrestrial causes by focusing on a universally acknowledged phenomenon. The fundamental problem is to determine whether, on a planetary scale, the marine regressions at the end of the Cretaceous had enough of a climatic impact to cause these series of extinctions on land and at sea. Changes in sea level, and sequences of marine transgressions and regressions on the Earth's surface—phenomena that were discovered long ago—are at the very heart of geology. The system of geological chronology in fact consists of a succession of episodes that begin with a marine transgression and end with a regression.

The magnitude of the terminal Cretaceous regressions was considerable, especially in the Maastrichtian, when sea level dropped almost 500 feet. An event like this would inevitably have led to climatic and ecological readjustments, which in turn affected life in the seas and on land. The pericontinental neritic zone that is home to much of the marine fauna would have shrunk considerably, and that might have spelled the end for the ammonites and belemnites. The climatic effects of the marine regressions were a drying and cooling trend, followed by warming. Such temperature changes might have been fatal to the dinosaurs, if we assume the dinosaurs were as sensitive to temperature as other reptiles. But in fact we have seen that the other groups of reptiles did not disappear at the K–T boundary: small animals, which we know to be capable of hibernating without permanent damage, exhibited more resistance. For example, the rhyn-chocephalians (similar to large lizards), a group that began to differentiate even before the dinosaurs first appeared, not only did not disappear, but is still present today: a relict species—the spotted spheno-don, or tuatara—lives on in New Zealand. And this living reptile has very little need for heat, remaining quite active even when the air temperature drops to 48°F. Turning to the seas, however, it seems much more difficult to explain the spectacular drop in the number of plankton species by a decrease in temper-ature. The Maastrichtian climate was subject to "pronounced seasonality," no doubt to an unprece-dented degree, but not to catastrophic cooling.

The most fascinating aspect of these extinction phenomena at the end of the Mesozoic is still the vul-nerability of the dinosaurs. Even if they were represented at the last by only a dozen species, why did all of them succumb? Were climatic conditions really so difficult? If the dinosaurs were bothered by the relatively cooler and drier climate, why did they not survive in tropical and equatorial regions, which were less affected by climatic variations? The mam-mals are believed to have passed through the K–T boundary with flying colors, thus ensuring a bright future for this most praiseworthy group (praisewor-thy because we belong to it). But a study of species representing this group associated with dinosaurs from the North American sites has shown that many species of mammals subsequently disappeared. It was the concurrent emergence of new species (which lived on into the Tertiary) that filled the "vacuums" created by the extinctions. That is why, at first glance, the mammals do not appear to have suffered the phenomenon of extinction. The dinosaurs of the final Maastrichtian, on the other hand, generated no speciation, no creation of new species.

The causes of these extinctions, with an infinite variety of magnitudes depending on the particular group, will be explained by research on paleobiological conditions. A research project of this kind is both more complex and less spectacular than positing the sudden, instantaneous arrival of an asteroid. I do not wish to rule out *a priori* the possibility of a meteoric impact at the end of the Cretaceous. But there can be no doubt that the dinosaurs, like probably most other groups that became extinct, were suffering at the end of the Maastrichtian from "ecological stress," to use the neat phrase coined by the American paleontologists William Clemens and David Archibald.

This ecological stress, associated with phenomena which predated the K–T boundary, is no longer ignored even by promoters of catastrophist theories: the suddenness with which an extraterrestrial body (asteroid or comet) strikes is apparently not as "sudden" as had been claimed. The catastrophist scenarios to which Walter Alvarez lent his support in 1987 assume that the extraterrestrial "event" produced mass extinctions for a period of more than three million years. One of the reasons for this about-face is that according to current thinking, the iridium deposit itself was less abrupt than had been believed, and might have lasted 500,000 years, as proposed by the French physicist Robert Rocchia.

According to the new catastrophist version of events, a rain of comets fell on the Earth for periods ranging from one to three million years, and this cometary spasm caused the various phases of extinction recorded during the Upper Cretaceous. This can be regarded as a compromise between the single, sudden impact hypothesis, and the so-called gradualist models, in which the extinctions took place over almost ten million years. The initial theory of an asteroid impact is still in favor with the media: much is made of explorations in search of the asteroid impact crater in the Yucatán in Mexico, or in the Caribbean south of Cuba, just as researchers are assuming that what actually struck the planet was a "cometary rain." The theory has been just as substantially modified by one of its major promoters.

Others—geochemists and geophysicists, including Vincent Courtillot in France—are turning to volcanoes in search of the ultimate cause of these extinctions. Contrary to previous belief, the iridium enrichment could have had a terrestrial source, attributable to an exceptionally high level of volcanism. The volcanoes of Hawaii and Réunion, for example, produce iridium. In the past, volcanism on this scale did indeed exist, in India. The Deccan Traps are an immense lava flow with an area bigger than that of France, and according to Courtillot and his co-workers, this Hawaiian type of fluid-lava volcanism occurred over a period of 500,000 years. But Hawaii's volcanoes do not inject substantial quantities of dust into the atmosphere, and this theory, unlike the cometary scenario, posits no cloud of dust to obscure the skies of Earth. Instead, the ocean surface became acidified by acid rains caused by sulfurous gas emissions, killing the plankton and producing climatic catastrophes. The only trouble is that not a trace of iridium has been identified in the Deccan lavas.

It appears that many things were happening in the Maastrichtian, and that any species which crossed the K–T boundary unscathed was fortunate indeed. Moreover, as I have mentioned with reference to mammals, we must not forget that although some species disappeared during the Maastrichtian, others also made their first appearance. According to calculations by Michael Benton concerning the vertebrates, eighteen new families of fishes appeared at this time, along with twenty-one tetrapod families: true pioneers.

The particular vulnerability of the last of the dinosaurs nevertheless remains a puzzle worth considering. What is still the best known of the Final

Cretaceous faunas is not only confined to North America, but is known primarily from one state, Montana. Extrapolations from these local data about the pace of dinosaur extinction on a global scale seem highly presumptuous. Meticulous research on sedimentation rates must also be conducted in the various Maastrichtian formations known throughout the world, to eliminate the bias introduced by sedimentation gaps. Accounting for the local effects of the great marine regressions, and determining the sequence of ecosystems at the end of the Cretaceous, represent long-term undertakings. An immense amount of paleontological work remains to be done, on a worldwide scale, before we can understand the mechanism underlying the extinctions at the end of the Cretaceous.

MASTODONS AND ECOLOGICAL STRESS

The need for a detailed study of paleobiological data can be illustrated by an example, on a totally different scale, that has been a very particular concern of mine: that of the disappearance, some ten thousand years ago, of a large mammal called the American mastodon, or *Mammut americanum* as it is known in the trade.

This species, known in North America for three and a half million years, belonged, just like modern elephants, to the order Proboscidea. It was the last representative of the mammutid family, first seen in Africa 22 million years ago. The skeleton of the American mastodon looks more robust, elongated, and low-slung than that of the elephant. A number of small-scale anatomical peculiarities make it possible to distinguish the skeletal remains of mastodons from those of elephants and, more particularly, from those of their contemporaries, the mammoths. The morphology of the molars is completely different: it is impossible, even for a novice, to misidentify the teeth of these animals.

With my colleague Jeffrey Saunders—an American paleontologist who, among his other discoveries, has brought to light an impressive number of these mastodons in Missouri—I looked at the evolution of these animals, whose molars had undergone very little change, compared to those of elephants, in 22 million years. The deposits excavated by Saunders did not yield just mastodons; a number of animal and plant species were discovered at the same time. Faunal and floral analyses made by Saunders and J. E. King were used to reconstruct a precise chronological sequence beginning 130,000 years ago. With this information, environmental changes over time have been studied in detail and compared with the fate of the American mastodon. In the Pleistocene (between 1.65 million and 10,000 years ago), a period characterized by numerous climatic oscillations, phases with a temperate or warm climate alternated with harsh glacial periods. In North America, the ice cap was centered on Hudson Bay. Advances and retreats of the ice sheet during the climatic swings were accompanied by profound changes in habitat. Open forests consisting of pines accompanied by deciduous trees (especially oaks) correspond to warmer phases, while forests dominated by spruce indicate very cold phases. It has been possible to track, in detail, the withdrawal of the tundras and the periglacial spruce forests which followed the retreat of the ice sheet, leaving behind immense periglacial lakes (most notably the present-day Great Lakes). In this region, an accurate narrative of the last 26,000 years allows us to follow, practically step by step, the fate of the American mastodon.

It appears that mastodons adapted particularly well to the rigorous climate of the glacial phases. They are found in abundance in the spruce forests, which represent its optimum habitat. The populations of *Mammut americanum* followed the retreat of these forests, which began to thin out in the Great Lakes region starting 15,000 years ago until a sudden climatic warming 12,000 years ago. The spruce forests acted as mastodon refuge areas within large expanses of less favorable habitat. We can therefore describe the last populations of mastodons as having an "insular" distribution; and when the last "islands" disappeared 11,000 years ago, the last of the mastodons vanished with them. The final warming replaced the spruce forests with forests of deciduous species, but in contrast to earlier climatic and ecological changes, which occurred at a pace that allowed for an adaptive response by the mastodons, events at the end of the Pleistocene happened too quickly for the adaptive process to express itself again.

This scenario, based largely on a very accurate understanding of the distribution of habitats during the final Pleistocene, attributes the extinction of the American mastodon to environmental insularity. In this case, intense ecological stress over a period of three to four thousand years is sufficient to explain the disappearance of a species. Although a rather short time span is involved, we certainly cannot speak of a catastrophic event: the last climatic fluctuations—on a scale of about a thousand years—were rapid but not instantaneous from a biological point of view. No such accuracy has yet been attained in assessing the evolution of habitats at the very end of the Cretaceous. If we could establish that the last dinosaurs disappeared over a period of 3,000 years, should we think of this as an instantaneous event simply because that event is so very remote from us? Whether 65 million years ago or 15,000 years ago, 3,000 years is still 3,000 years.

I do not cite this example to imply, by analogy, that the dinosaurs also fell victim to environmental insularity. I simply want to emphasize the complexity of the biological phenomena that can influence the fate of animal populations. The dinosaurs are no exception to this rule.

Dozens of genera of mammals disappeared at the end of the Pleistocene; these extinctions, marking the end of the glaciations, have been referred to as the "prehistoric revolution." Let's say all the large mammals of the Ice Age had been classified in a single group, perhaps because of their extraordinary size. With the American mastodon, the mammoth, the cave lion, cave bear, cave hyena, giant tundra stag, woolly rhinoceros, giant ground sloth, and a number of specifically American mammals, it would be easy to equal and exceed the number of final Cretaceous dinosaurs found in North America. An entire group would have been snuffed out instantaneously in the Upper Pleistocene: a major event.

The example may seem strained, but this sort of caricature does have its relevance to the problem of the end of the dinosaurs. The extinction of a taxonomic group makes sense only if the group is a natural one, in other words if it contains species which share a single genealogical history. But if we want to regard the dinosaurs as a natural group, we should include birds, too—they are the descendants of small, fleet-footed carnivorous dinosaurs of the Jurassic period. We cannot label a natural group "extinct" if one of its branches displays a high level of evolutionary dynamism, which the birds certainly do. The fact that this branch is generally classified separately from the dinosaurs for various reasons (the principal one being that zoological groups, as classified, are not necessarily natural), makes no difference. From a strictly genealogical point of view the dinosaurs are not extinct, because they still exist as birds. Although this purely logical argument is flawless, it will not convince anyone, because what corresponds to the standard image of a dinosaur has indeed disappeared.

It is undoubtedly because the dinosaurs represent one of the great myths of modern times that the question of their disappearance is so universally fascinating. Nobody cares about what happened to the plankton, or to *Inoceramus*, or, conversely, about the well-being of the champsosaurs or even the fate of any particular species of dinosaur—*Pachycephalosaurus wyomingensis* or *Ankylosaurus magniventris*. No, what matters is the extinction of the archetypal Dinosaur, the monster that has taken the place in our imagination of the dragons of the Old Days. Whatever the arguments of the paleontologists about taxonomy or the tempo of extinctions, that Dinosaur has disappeared completely.

The revival of this question, which is almost as old as the first identification of the dinosaurs, has been subtly and effectively linked to another: the irresistible allure of space and extraterrestrial phenomena, and the verdict of physics, a science that stands above all reproach. In the 1980s, when the Big Bang was all the rage, everything came from space: both life (amino acids hitchhiking on a meteorite) and death (the comet that killed the dinosaurs). The asteroid theory had, moreover, been preceded in the late 1960s by the supernova theory, which enjoyed its heyday during the 1970s: it stated that a supernova explosion had decimated the dinosaurs by bombarding them with x-rays and ultraviolet radiation. The asteroid theory was more successful, no doubt because of the prestige of Luis Alvarez, a Nobel laureate in physics. In his writings, Alvarez made no secret of his belief that the work of physicists was intrinsically superior: among other good qualities, physicists possessed the ability to reason and experiment. Alvarez did not hesitate to state in 1983 that there was now proof that the asteroid had fallen, and that it had had a disastrous effect on *life in the oceans*; he also compared skeptics to geologists who, despite all the evidence, still refused to acknowledge the reality of continental drift. The paleontologists, desperately clinging to a gradualist vision of geological phenomena, were to him decidedly out of date. But it was from the physicists, as we have seen, that the first contradictions came. The iridium enrichment at the end of the Cretaceous took much longer, they said; another iridium level was soon identified and dated to 2.3 million years ago

(Pliocene), and it was not associated with any mass extinction.

But the American paleontologists David Raup and John Sepkoski went further than anyone else. They analyzed the distribution of all the identified families of marine animals dating back to the Cambrian, based on the compendium drawn up by Sepkoski in 1982. The result, published in 1984, was an unexpected chronology of mass extinctions: they had occurred on Earth every 26 million years. This sort of regularity could only have been caused by cosmic factors! The theory attracted its adherents, but also its detractors (fairly convincing ones to my way of thinking), who based their objections on both statistics and taxonomy. The British paleontologists Colin Patterson and Andrew Smith, for example, showed that with regard to fish and echinoderms (sea urchins and starfish)—the groups whose evolution the researchers had respectively studied—only 25% of the postulated extinctions involved natural groups and could in that sense be considered real. Their highly critical conclusion was that the periodicity was nothing but background noise (at least for the two groups they examined). Nor did the terrestrial forms confirm Raup and Sepkoski's hypothesis. It is true that a number of periods of mass (but not necessarily instantaneous) extinction have been identified throughout Earth's history. The most important of these came at the end of the Permian, 245 million years ago, when Sepkoski estimated that almost 90% of marine species disappeared (which immediately makes the mass extinction at the end of the Cretaceous look quite modest). But the central thesis, the regularity of these phenomena, remains to be proven. Moreover, subsequent to some closely reasoned statistical discussions, Raup and Sepkoski concluded elegantly in 1988 that the hypothesis of periodic extinctions was based on statistical inferences drawn from muddled data, so that it could neither be proved nor disproved in a truly satisfactory manner. I could not have put it better myself.

This quick survey of diversification, adaptation, and extinction naturally suggests a simple conclusion concerning the random nature of history. The relativity of the idea of adaptation, the phenomenon of mass extinctions, and, as a general rule, the evolutionary scenarios that have emerged from phylogenetic investigations, do not corroborate the notion of "progress." Perhaps the marine regressions at the end of the Cretaceous were sufficient to cool down the climate, or maybe an asteroid or a rain of comets brought about these climatic upheavals; the specific mechanism essentially has nothing to do with the question of whether the survivors were "better adapted," or the losers were for some reason inferior.

One last example is cited by Stephen Jay Gould: We have seen that the plankton was decimated during the Maastrichtian, but not everything disappeared. Diatoms, plant members of the plankton, did pass through the Cretaceous–Tertiary boundary. We know that when conditions become unfavorable and food sources become scarce, diatoms change their morphology, turn into spores with a "frozen" metabolism, and sink into the depths. Perhaps, says Gould, it was this ability that allowed them to survive, unscathed, the climatic perturbations of the final Cretaceous—especially if the "nuclear winter" model proves to be the correct one. But whatever the case, the ability to change form cannot be equated with progress; those members of the plankton that became extinct were not therefore "inferior" to the ones that managed to survive. Speaking of the Paleozoic era extinctions, Gould states that there is not the slightest proof— not even the shadow of any proof—that the losers in the great decimation were systematically inferior to the survivors in terms of their anatomical organization.

It is easy to understand that the hypothesis of an extraterrestrial agent for the Cretaceous mass extinction is particularly attractive to anyone who, like Gould, mistrusts the idea of evolutionary progress. Gould states, with characteristic directness: "I need hardly say that if a mass extinction operates like a genuine lottery, with each group holding a ticket unrelated to its anatomical virtues, then contingency

[... has] been proven."[*] And to our way of thinking, nothing could indeed be more random than the impact of a meteorite; this blind bombardment makes nonsense of any claimed adaptive inequalities among species. But I hope the reader will have understood that for a paleontologist like myself, the specifics of the Great Dying at the end of the Cretaceous, and during the other mass extinction periods—questions like Who disappeared? When? At what pace?—are pivotal, and answers to them can be gained only by studying the fossils. In sum, the popular success of a scientific idea must not become the major criterion for selecting research topics; otherwise we risk sliding into science fiction, or at least into science as entertainment.

---

[*] S. J. Gould, *Wonderful Life*, New York, W. W. Norton, 1989, p. 306.

IV

THE LAST

MESSAGE

Researchers today are often hesitant to discuss an essential aspect of their profession: pleasure. The image of the researcher—hunched over a sink or a microscope, occasionally touching a few keys to commune imperturbably with the computer, and most often swathed in a white lab coat—creates an atmosphere of gravity that would seem to exclude any element of play. Having fun does not seem to be a concept given much emphasis in research reports. But research is also an act of creation, in which enjoyment must necessarily find a place; and paleontology is no exception to this rule. Even though research is less and less frequently explained as a simple process of expanding knowledge (although that idea will probably never become completely obsolete), we must remember that without the pleasure of searching and finding, there would have been very few breakthroughs in basic research. Paleontological research can certainly be justified by the need to date landforms to pave the way for petroleum exploration, or to conserve our heritage (the archives of the planet), but the essential aspect of the paleontologist's work, as far as I am concerned, is still the pleasure of discovery.

THE PALEONTOLOGIST'S DELIGHT

Evolution is full of surprises. We now know a great deal about the history of life that Lamarck, Cuvier, and Darwin never knew. But we might just as well admit that we know nothing about it, if we think about the torrent of historical events that have produced the evolution of tens of millions of species over the three and a half billion years since life first appeared on Earth.

Discovering anatomical arrangements that were hitherto unknown, or solving a problem concerning the evolutionary tempo or genealogical affinities of some particular group—these are part of the paleontologist's ultimate delight. Constructing a phylogenetic problem—what is called, in the cladistic jargon, building a "cladogram"—is no easy matter. There are more than two million combinations to be considered in drawing up a dichotomous tree for the relationships among only nine species. A laborious examination of the characteristics possessed by each species finally leads, occasionally with some help from the computer, to the discovery of a solution that optimally interprets the observations. A fragment of the history of life has thus emerged. That moment brings an intense, silent, and solitary satisfaction. Yes indeed, researchers can be monumental egotists!

The discovery of fossils is a pleasure that cannot be described as fundamental, but I will not underestimate its importance. It is the paleontologist's first delight, shared with every amateur fossilhound. Who can deny that bringing to light the remains of a being that lived millions of years before the emergence of Wise Humans—*Homo sapiens*—represents a fresh surprise every time? But professionals—whose final purpose, after all, is to expand knowledge rather than accumulate objects—find another dimension in the search for fossils: the excavation itself. Modern paleontological excavation techniques, borrowed for the most part from methods developed by archeologists, now have little in common with the practices of the first paleontologists. Scalpels and paintbrushes are used far more often than pickaxes. Techniques are particularly delicate in vertebrate paleontology, since the fossil remains of vertebrates are both rarer and more difficult to extract from the ground than those of invertebrates. Every specimen counts. In the field, a bone (and especially a skeleton) poses much more difficult problems than a shell.

A paleontological excavation can certainly be regarded as an environmentally destructive undertaking: where once there was a grassy hill or a sheer canyon, now there is nothing but a bare gash from which fossil bones have been extracted. In order not to be accused of vandalism, paleontologists must provide to the scientific institutions who finance them the totality of their discoveries. This totality is a dual one: all of the scientific information, which must appear in the form of publications, and all of the objects themselves. Totality rhymes with integrity, and the fossils must be delivered just as they were discovered: excavation must not aggravate the natural ravages of time. In public collections, whether exhibited or kept in storage for exclusively scientific consultation, fossils must appear just as they appeared to the excavator. That is why excavation techniques today are highly sophisticated.

Long ago, the paleontologist paid laborers to keep exposing fresh scarps. When a fossil appeared, all of it—or more often, what was left of it—was brought to the paleontologist. If the scientist was actually on the site he or she would examine it; if it was considered useful, it was packed up and shipped to the laboratory for study. Those days are long gone. Today, in many cases for lack of funds (although one must sometimes make a virute of necessity), the researcher does everything: handling the pick, shovel, trowel, hammer and chisel, scalpel, paintbrush, needle, and a variety of dental instruments for really delicate work. Discovering fossils has become almost an artistic pursuit. There is undeniably a certain beauty in the arrangement of fossil bones exhumed little by little, still in the position where they lay when ultimately buried: ancient ground reappears after millions of years. Preparing a fossil *in situ* is both an aesthetic and a scientific pleasure. It requires solutions to technical problems that depend on the nature of the sediment and the solidity of the fossil itself, to the extent that one can identify what has been found. That is why today, a visit to an excavation site does not involve clambering over heaps of sand or gravel; instead it reveals an ancient landscape, a lake, marsh, riverbed, or meander, yielding up its fossils like a page of history slowly being deciphered.

The aesthetic pleasure of a "beautiful" site therefore meets a scientific need. Truth and beauty are combined in it, because the only way to determine deposition and fossilization conditions, and to define how the skeletal remains accumulated, is to conduct a clean and precise excavation. That alone will provide information about the significance of the fossil-bearing deposit: instantaneous deposition, progressive accumulation over time, irregular accumulation, or disturbance of the fossils before they were definitively buried. Everything is recorded, and the position of each fossil is marked on the site plan. The time when one selected the good-looking specimens, or the ones that seemed *a priori* significant, is gone. All this information is used to determine whether the bias introduced by random factors in fossilization is substantial, whether the sample represents the entire fauna that lived during that period, or perhaps a specific, restricted biotope. The rapidly developing science of taphonomy seeks to reveal these deposition conditions, investigating the connections between a fossil and its environment in minute detail: type of sediment, placement of fossils, even breaks or other marks on them.

But finding a "good piece" is still an unparalleled delight. I have hunted mastodons all over the world, from France to Pakistan, Israel to Bulgaria, but the nicest specimens I ever discovered were the closest to home, dug up from the sunny hillsides of southern France. The discovery of my first large fossil, seventeen years ago almost to the day as I write this, is still a precious memory.

Beneath the wheat fields of the Simorre region of southern France, paleontologists can find remains of the large mammals that lived in our country about fifteen million years ago. The sediments deposited by the great rivers that flowed down from the Pyrenees at that time were effective "fossil traps"; under the wheat lie the beaches, or more precisely the river sands and gravels with their fossil bones. We had been digging for several days in fine sand at a locality called En Péjouan, without making any major discoveries, when my trowel struck a hard object that gleamed in the sun as soon as I brushed it off. A flat, perfectly smooth surface of reddish-brown enamel appeared; beyond any doubt, I had just found a mastodon tusk.

Tusks are incisors that grow continuously. Like the incisors of any mammal, those of the first proboscideans were covered with enamel above the ivory. As evolution proceeded, the enamel became progressively thinner until it disappeared in modern elephants. The tusks of very young elephants are actually still covered with enamel, since enamel must be produced to allow the tooth to form and then erupt. But once the incisor is in place, enamel production very soon stops, which is why ivory is visible over the entire surface of an elephant's tusks. In the mastodons that I was hoping to discover, enamel persisted in adults in the form of a lateral band. With two brushstrokes I had uncovered the top of the tusk with the entire width of the enamel band: it was an adult tusk. I worked towards the back of the specimen, and found that it was not a fragment but a whole tusk, or at least most of one. I photographed the object exactly as I had found it.

But I was not interested in discovering just isolated teeth: mastodon tusks and molars are not uncommon in natural history museums. My stated goal was an intact skull—infinitely more rare. In primitive mastodons, the tusks point downward and outward and the enamel band twists around the tusk in a beautiful spiral: it is ventral at the front and lateral at mid-length. As it had emerged, my specimen was evidently a right-hand tusk, seen from the ventral side. I immediately set to work with a brush, clearing the area where the left tusk should be if, by good fortune, I had found a skull. A tusk tip, perfectly symmetrical, appeared. My jubilation was hard to contain; but the definitive proof was missing: the molars. Tusks, together with a palate, inevitably implied the presence of a completely preserved cranium. Just where the molars ought to have been... the excavation area ended.

The deposit was located on a hillside in a sloping field, facing directly southwest. We had brought in a backhoe to remove the wheatfield and reach the sandy fossil-bearing stratum, which was horizontal. An area of 100 square meters had been prepared and, thanks to the rare understanding of the landowner, we were able to work on land that, in principle, was set aside for agriculture. My discovery was located in the southeast corner of the site, where the sandy fossil-bearing layer was covered by almost six feet of topsoil. I feverishly swept away the sandy layer at the base of the scarp, and there were the molars: first the right second molar, then the left. It was indeed a complete skull. The two molars were heavily worn, so we had in fact found an adult.

A short explanation: it has been found that molar rank can be used to determine the age of an individual elephant or mastodon. Unlike other mammals (and the most primitive proboscideans), in a mastodon the premolars and molars are not all present together throughout the animal's life: after they erupt and are worn down, the teeth are shed one after another. When the last molar (the third, or wisdom tooth) comes in, the premolars have been shed, the first molars are very worn or have also been shed, and the second molars are worn. The process is the same in elephants, but is even more simplified: the premolars have disappeared, and the molars follow one another over the course of the individual's life. The sequence for each half-jaw is: three "baby" molars—not replaced by premolars—and three permanent molars. The frontmost molars that I had uncovered were the second molars, and they were worn: therefore they belonged to an adult.

There was great celebration on the site, but very quickly we had to face facts: removing this skull would mean cutting back the scarp. After protecting what had been exposed, we set to work with pick and shovel, attacking the three or four feet of topsoil that lay above the fossil-bearing layer. The village mayor, who had come to see how the excavation was progressing, even lent a hand—he was leaving the next day, and absolutely had to see what this ancient skull looked like. But the job turned out to be a long one, and night fell before we saw any more of the mastodon. Next day we called in the backhoe again, and expanded the site towards the southeast. Excavations in the fossil layer resumed, and slowly the outline of the cranium appeared. The palate was completely preserved, with the last molars still in place. The base of the rear of the skull, with the auditory regions, was missing. The skull had come to rest upside down, and in classic fashion, as it was being buried fifteen million years ago, the part of the skull that had been above ground the longest wore away and then vanished under the action of erosion.

Little by little the skull was consolidated with liquid adhesive, then covered with glue-soaked paper and "plastered." One advantage of sand is that it is easy to dig in, but often the fossils found in it are poorly mineralized and very fragile, especially if there is considerable runoff. Fossil bones are wet, extremely fragile, and impossible to remove *in situ*. A shell then has to be constructed around the specimen, using strips of cloth soaked in plaster. The fossil, imprisoned in this protective cocoon, is then turned over (a tricky operation: if the plastering job is incomplete, the specimen falls out and is destroyed) and taken away. My colleague Christian de Muizon and I set off for the neighboring farms to scrounge old pieces of metal as reinforcement for the plaster. We spent days working on the cocoon. When we were done the plaster-encased skull was turned over: not an easy job, but no damage was done. That was the real occasion for celebration: we all knew that nothing else could happen to our precious specimen. We suspended it on a chain from the bucket of a backhoe, and lifted it into a truck that carried off the results of our excavation season. The entire object (skull, sediment, and plaster) weighed almost 1,500 pounds.

The entire assemblage was then completely uncovered in the laboratory, at the Muséum National d'Histoire Naturelle in Paris. It was a second excavation, this time looking for the top of the skull. Working with fine needles mounted in handles, we were able to distinguish every detail of the bone surface. As the bones emerged, I began to see the structure of the nasal fossae, the orbits, and the premaxillaries that housed the massive tusks.

The species to which this skull belonged had first been identified by Cuvier, in 1806, on the basis of teeth found in this very same Simorre region: he called it the "narrow-toothed" mastodon. Its history is therefore bound up with that of vertebrate paleontology itself. Cuvier knew the species only from isolated teeth, however, since no skull had ever been described. For more than two centuries, the Simorre region had been famous for yielding fossils: we had not come there by accident. A few decades ago, farmers following behind their ox-drawn plows would easily distinguish the fossils turned up by their plowshares as they encountered the horizontal fossil-bearing layer (at an elevation of about 920–980 feet) cropping out here and there depending on the slope of the hills. The huge mastodon molars and tusk fragments were impossible to overlook, and it is not unusual to see such molars (called "giants' teeth") on farmhouse chimneys throughout this region. Some farmers still remember finding fossils when they were children, or recall the place where their father said he had found molars, or simply had gone to dig up sand. One particular—and always delightful—aspect of fossil-hunting on cultivated land, where practically nothing remains above the surface, is that a great deal depends on human relations. In arid landscapes, on the other hand, like Pakistan or the Rift Valley of East Africa, it is only after long treks into ravines and natural cuttings that bones are found, brought to light by erosion; that is the only way to discover fossil-bearing sites that are worth a major excavation project.

My mastodon skull, along with several others, was put on public display as part of an exhibit organized by the Musée en Herbe and the Muséum National d'Histoire Naturelle at the Jardin d'Acclimatation in Paris. The purpose of the exhibit was to explain evolution to younger audiences, based on familiar animals: the elephants and their ancestors. Without realizing it, these children saw things that Cuvier had never seen, and took it in stride. Fossils are no longer surprising, and that is a good thing: we know now that fossils are not fantasies, and that life has a history.

The excavations in Gers and Haute-Garonne, very nearby in southern France, continued for eleven consecutive years. At the En Péjouan site alone, we found mastodon remains belonging to about twenty individuals, from newborns to old adults, and I discovered in the process that the females, which were much smaller than the males, had very small tusks or none at all. The purpose of the research program that formed the context of these expeditions in the shadow of the Pyrenees was to define the chronological succession of mammalian faunas in sedimentary basins north of the Tethys Sea. As we have seen with reference to primates, the role of the Tethys in the diversification of mammalian faunas has been—and still is—of enormous interest. Specialists meet regularly, at conferences, round tables, and other symposia, to compare their results and refine the chronology of their deposits and geographical reconstructions—what we call biostratigraphy and paleobiogeography. But that is another story, one that takes us away from southern hillsides and the domain of simple pleasure.

THE NECESSITY OF FOSSILS

There is no longer any need to fight for the idea that fossils are genuine, and that biological evolution is a reality. The battle waged by the American creationist sects is out of step with the times and with reason.

So what is the use of finding a few more fossils? Don't we keep hearing that the museums are already full? Surely the general outlines of the history of evolution—phylogeny—are already well understood? Are there not other fields of study like genes, much newer and much closer to the intimate structure of living matter, that should engage those who want to understand biological evolution? Shouldn't paleontologists be restrained from having fun by discovering "beautiful objects," as one particularly rash member of the profession has just admitted?

You will not expect me, of course, to answer all these questions in the affirmative. Throughout this little book, I have tried to present some of the scientific questions that are being asked about evolution, none of which can be answered without the information supplied by fossils. We have just seen that even when a fossil species has been identified for two centuries, absolutely new information can still be discovered. Entire groups are known to us only by certain types of characteristics, especially teeth in the case of mammals. As soon as true skeletal material is found, evolutionary conclusions will need to be refined or even completely reversed. The evolution of characteristics in different directions and at different paces—"mosaic evolution"—is a fundamental process which gives us one of the keys to the evolutionary mechanism in general and adaptation in particular. We have also seen that investigations of evolutionary tempo, the roles played by gradualist and punctuated processes, require the discovery of very large numbers of fossils, and a remarkably dense and accurate stratigraphic record. The answer to the question, therefore, is that there are far more topics for future study than topics already studied. We have also seen the wealth of information provided by fossils in support of paleogeographic reconstructions. For periods during the Paleozoic era, models derived from plate tectonics are infinitely less precise than for later periods. In this case fossils represent invaluable vectors for paleogeographic inferences, and for the reconstruction of ancient continents and oceans—just as they were in Wegener's time for the reconstruction of Gondwanaland.

The work that might be described as routine, like the great monographs that present exhaustive studies of some taxonomic group, or the fauna of a particular period in a particular region, are the very foundation of extrapolations at a general level. They often lead to profound changes in what were thought to be established facts. The history of the punctuated equilibrium model sums up this aspect of the discipline all by itself: without specifically paleontological monographs about terrestrial snails and marine trilobites, ontogenic models of heterochronic development and the actualist model of geographic speciation would never have been tested—and nurtured—in the light of history.

In reality, if we want to illustrate the history of life over time, we need more and more fossils to fill in the gaps. The archives of the Earth are continually being enriched, but there are still considerable empty spots. For example, no tetrapods have ever been discovered from the Aalenian stage of the Jurassic (between 175 and 180 million years ago). The Jurassic, between 200 and 130 million years ago, although it was the golden age of the dinosaurs, is still a period that has been globally stingy with fossil remains of terrestrial vertebrates. If we want to understand the history of life over time, we need more and more fossils: this time to refine the problems confronting anyone who wishes to comprehend the tempo of evolution and the biogeographical distributions of the past.

Illustrating and understanding: these two aspects of the study of biological evolution in its historical dimension are inseparable. What really happened on Earth cannot be perceived, or even approximated, without fossils. They are an essential check on models often based on present-day reality. As historians of life, paleontologists are interested not so much in what might have happened given the probability of a certain evolutionary event based on a certain model, but in deciphering the actual past, and reconstructing the single history that governed the development of life for almost four billion years. Of course, as we have already seen, decipherment and reconstruction do not come immediately. History cannot be read directly from the rocks, and we must apply a theoretical filter to our observations; otherwise paleontology would not be a science. But as it happens, our raw material—and this is an extraordinary stroke of luck—comes to us with no distortion other than the changes caused by erosion and the processes of fossilization: by time, in a word. Given the amount of information imparted, these changes are by far a lesser evil.

Like all the disciplines of systematics—that venerable science that studies biological diversity over time and space—paleontology has never been conceptually better equipped than in the late 20th century. But it also seems that its place among the sciences has never been so precarious. A single example, taken from outside France to spare our domestic sensibilities (and careers): last year, the Fossil Mammals section was eliminated in a reorganization of one of the greatest, if not the greatest, natural history museums in the world, the British Museum (Natural History) in London. Some think that paleontologists—evolutionary historians, and as such bowed down by the weight of years—are out of fashion. They have said everything there is to say, and can therefore be dispensed with. They are themselves on the road to extinction. I often have conversations with people who are surprised to learn that paleontologists still exist. Geology students wonder whether it is sensible to continue on such a risky career track, and other students, future biologists, even seem amazed to learn that there are still major paleontological field expeditions working all over the world! But as we have seen, researchers today are constructing a new theory of macroevolution that puts all its emphasis on each of the various levels of integration of evolutionary phenomena. One of these levels is that of the organism, in both its taxonomic and chronological aspects. The fossil is merely one of the components that make up geological strata. Evolution does not operate simply at the level of transcription errors in DNA nucleotide sequences.

Many questions that have emerged from the fossil archives have not even been touched on here, and the scientific challenges that face the paleontologist have never been as numerous or as promising. The theory of evolution that emerged in the Thirties and Forties has very appropriately been called the Synthetic Theory, for every evolutionary discipline has a place in it. But the lure of reductionism has always existed, and that temptation still persists today. Could the paleontologists end up sending the last message from the fossils? I hope not: three billion years of history is worth at least a handful of paleontologists, and maybe even more.

BIBLIOGRAPHY

ALLEN, K. C. and D. E. G. BRIGGS (eds.), *Evolution and the Fossil Record*, Washington, DC, Smithsonian Institution, 1989.

DE BONIS, L., *Évolution et extinction dans le règne animal* [Evolution and extinction in the animal kingdom], Paris, Masson, 1991.

COPPENS, Y., *Le Singe, l'Afrique, et l'Homme* [Apes, Africa, and humans], Paris, Fayard, 1983.

DAVID, B., J.-L. DOMMERGUES, J. CHALINE, and B. LAURIN (coordinators), *Ontogenèse et Évolution* [Ontogenesis and evolution], Géobios Mém. Sp. 12, Lyon, 1989.

DEVILLERS, C. and J. CHALINE, *La Théorie de l'évolution* [The theory of evolution], Paris, Dunod, 1989.

ELDREDGE, N., *Time Frames*, New York, Simon & Schuster, 1985.

Collection of authors: *Les Extinctions dans l'histoire des vertébrés* [Extinctions in the history of the vertebrates], Mémoires de la Société géologique de France, No. 150, Paris, 1987.

GOULD, S. J., *Hen's Teeth and Horse's Toes*, New York, W. W. Norton, 1983.

GOULD, S. J., *Wonderful Life*, New York, W. W. Norton, 1989.

HUBLIN, J.-J. and A.-M. TILLIER (eds.), *Aux origines d'*Homo sapiens [The origins of *Homo sapiens*], Paris, PUF, 1991.

LAURENT, G., *Paléontologie et évolution en France, 1800–1860* [Paleontology and evolution in France, 1800–1860], Paris, publications of the Comité des travaux historiques et scientifiques, 1987.

Collection of authors: *On a marché sur la terre* [Walking on the Earth], Paris, ICS/Muséum national d'histoire naturelle, 1991.

Collection of authors: *La Recherche en paléontologie* [Paleontological research], Paris, Le Seuil, "Points Sciences" series, 1989.

TASSY, P. (coordinator), *L'Ordre et la diversité du vivant* [Order and diversity in life], Paris, Fayard/ Fondation Diderot, 1986.

TASSY, P., *L'Arbre à remonter le temps* [Climbing the tree of time], Paris, Bourgois, 1991.

TAYLOR, P. D. and G. P. LARWOOD (eds.), *Major Evolutionary Radiations*, Oxford, Clarendon Press, 1990.

WEISHAMPEL, D. B., P. DODSON, and H. OSMOLKA, *The Dinosauria*, Berkeley, University of California Press, 1990.